MW01055010

CONNECTING THROUGH LEADERSHIP

The Promise of Precise and Effective Communication in Schools

Jasmine K. KULLAR

Solution Tree | Press

a division of
Solution Tree

Copyright © 2020 by Solution Tree Press

Materials appearing here are copyrighted. With one exception, all rights are reserved. Readers may reproduce only those pages marked "Reproducible." Otherwise, no part of this book may be reproduced or transmitted in any form or by any means (electronic, photocopying, recording, or otherwise) without prior written permission of the publisher.

555 North Morton Street
Bloomington, IN 47404
800.733.6786 (toll free) / 812.336.7700
FAX: 812.336.7790

email: info@SolutionTree.com
SolutionTree.com
Visit **go.SolutionTree.com/leadership** to download the free reproducibles in this book.

Printed in the United States of America

Library of Congress Cataloging-in-Publication Data

Names: Kullar, Jasmine K., 1976- author.
Title: Connecting through leadership : the promise of precise and effective communication in schools / Jasmine K. Kullar.
Description: Bloomington, IN : Solution Tree Press, [2020] | Includes bibliographical references and index.
Identifiers: LCCN 2019024107 (print) | LCCN 2019024108 (ebook) | ISBN 9781949539417 (paperback) | ISBN 9781949539424 (ebook)
Subjects: LCSH: Communication in education. | Educational leadership. | Teacher-administrator relationships. | Teacher-student relationships.
Classification: LCC LB1033.5 .K85 2020 (print) | LCC LB1033.5 (ebook) | DDC 371.102/2--dc23
LC record available at https://lccn.loc.gov/2019024107
LC ebook record available at https://lccn.loc.gov/2019024108

Solution Tree
Jeffrey C. Jones, CEO
Edmund M. Ackerman, President

Solution Tree Press
President and Publisher: Douglas M. Rife
Associate Publisher: Sarah Payne-Mills
Art Director: Rian Anderson
Managing Production Editor: Kendra Slayton
Production Editor: Miranda Addonizio
Content Development Specialist: Amy Rubenstein
Copy Editor: Kate St. Ives
Proofreader: Sarah Ludwig
Cover and Text Designer: Rian Anderson
Editorial Assistant: Sarah Ludwig

Acknowledgments

Thank you to my entire family for their support, understanding, and encouragement in everything that I do. To my husband Balraj and my amazing children, Sabrina and Dillon: you are my everything, and I dedicate this book to you. I so appreciated the late nights you stayed up with me to keep me company and, of course, the little celebrations along the way during the writing of this book. I love you always!

Thank you to my Solution Tree family. It has been an amazing journey, and I am so humbled and blessed to be a part of this work. Thank you to all my associate friends—I am so lucky to have so many intelligent and dedicated professionals I can call friends. Thank you to the entire Solution Tree staff for making this project feel so doable. Claudia Wheatley: I don't know what I'd do without our talks. Jeff Jones: I can't thank you enough for your incredible leadership and what you do for educators.

I will forever be grateful to Rick and Becky DuFour. I will always be thankful that they had confidence in me and allowed me to be a part of this amazing work. I hope this book contributes in some way to building stronger leaders so they can excel in doing the right work for all our students.

Solution Tree Press would like to thank the following reviewers:

Libby Bonesteel
Superintendent
Montpelier Roxbury Public Schools
Montpelier, Vermont

Cindy Hicks-Rodriguez
Principal
Brookvale Elementary School
Fremont, California

Kaua Matthews
Principal
Bosque Farms Elementary
Los Lunas, New Mexico

Visit **go.SolutionTree.com/leadership** to download
the free reproducibles in this book.

Table of Contents

Reproducible pages are in italics.

CHAPTER 4
Communicating Through Writing . . . 85

About the Author

Jasmine K. Kullar, EdD, is an assistant superintendent for Cobb County School District, the second-largest school district in Georgia. She is also a faculty member in the College of Professional Studies Educational Leadership Department at Albany State University in Georgia. In addition, she is involved with the Wallace Foundation's University Principal Preparation Initiative (UPPI) and a member of the national UPPI Professional Learning Community, focused on redesigning university educational leadership preparation programs.

Prior to these roles, she was a middle school principal for seven years at two separate schools. With over ten years of school leadership experience, Dr. Kullar has worked at the elementary, middle, and high school levels. She has taught in both Canada and the United States, giving her a variety of experiences in working with schools and school districts. She has expertise in building professional learning communities (PLCs) as well as school leadership.

Her experience with PLCs began in her first year of teaching, when she attended a PLC workshop and heard Rick DuFour. Since then, she has been implementing those tenets. When she became a school administrator, she led her school to Model PLC status—the first school to receive this designation in the state of Georgia. Her school's success as a PLC is featured on AllThingsPLC.info as "Sample Professional Learning Community Manual."

She has published articles with the Association for Supervision and Curriculum Development and presented several workshops at both the state and national levels. She is a lifelong learner, with her latest certificate from Harvard University in Leading School Systems at the National Level. She earned her doctorate degree from Argosy University in Georgia, her master's degree from Memorial University of Newfoundland, her teaching certificate from Medaille College in Buffalo, and her undergraduate degree from the University of Toronto.

Introduction

The art of communication is the language of leadership.

—James Humes

As a school leader, your job depends heavily on effective communication skills. Everything that leaders do requires communication skills—whether it's navigating a crisis, giving out directions, resolving conflict, or solving problems. Unfortunately, many leaders do not spend enough time strengthening this skill. Think about the workshops or conferences you attend; chances are they weren't on improving your communication skills. Yet all the workshops and conferences you have attended require strong communication skills in order for you to implement any of your new learning from those events.

I remember when I attended my first Professional Learning Community at Work® institute and learned about all kinds of things: prioritizing standards, grading and assessment, creating interventions, building a guiding coalition—and so on. My biggest challenge was figuring out how I was going to take all that new knowledge and learning and communicate it to my teachers. One mistake in my communication, and I wouldn't convey this important knowledge effectively. I personally have seen great ideas fail because of ineffective communication. I remember rolling out a writing across the curriculum initiative in which all teachers, regardless of what they taught, would incorporate writing into their day-to-day lessons. But when I observed the teachers, I didn't see that happening. It was easy to get upset with the teachers for not doing what I asked; however, when I self-reflected, I realized my communication about this initiative was incredibly weak. I didn't do a good job explaining, I tried to do too much via email instead of face to face, I didn't communicate examples of what I was looking for—all in all, what I wanted to see happen didn't happen because of my inability to communicate effectively. The good news is that these mistakes are easy to avoid.

Anchal Luthra and Richa Dahiya (2015) stress that without excellent communication skills, a leader simply cannot be effective. The success of your school can rise or fall based on your communication skills. Why are leadership and communication so connected? Leadership guru John C. Maxwell (1993) asserts, "When the leader lacks confidence, the followers lack commitment" (p. 6). This is undoubtedly true, and the only way to convey confidence is through effective communication skills. Through effective communication, you can show your teachers and staff members the way and influence them to commit to and excel in the essential work they do every day.

The answer, in short, is that without communicating, leaders cannot influence their followers. Leadership and communication are deeply connected, and successful leadership depends on successful communication. This book explores that connection, and how you can develop it to, in turn, connect with others and be an effective leader in your school.

The Importance of Communication

You communicate in multiple ways every single day. You communicate verbally through presentations, meetings, and conversations; you communicate through writing; and you communicate nonverbally through your body language. From the moment you walk into your school to the moment you leave, you are communicating. Deborah J. Barrett (2014) states, "A leader must be able to communicate effectively. When asked to define leadership, theorists and practitioners alike frequently use the words 'influence,' 'inspire,' and 'transform,' all of which depend on communication, verbal and nonverbal" (p. 2).

Not only do you communicate every day, you communicate with *a lot* of people. How many people in the school community do you lead? Or, how many people do you communicate with? The answer to both questions is the same. With just the teachers, staff members, students, and one parent per student, for a school or school district of about five hundred students, it could be well over one thousand people. And this number does not include visitors or a second parent. So, with that many people that you lead and, therefore, communicate with, it makes sense to ensure that your communication skills are effective, whether that's by building new skills, adapting the communication skills you used in your teaching days, or brushing up on skills you've already established.

Gary Burnison (2012) asserts that communication is about connection. Through effective communication, you build relationships, which leads to trust. You build relationships with your staff, teachers, parents, and students one at a time through your communication skills. When you call parents to tell them something positive about their child—you are building trust. When you give parents reassurance after something bad happens in your building—you are building trust. When you help teachers through a difficult parent meeting—you are building trust. When you support teachers through a tough time—you are building trust. Again—in every situation when you communicate with your stakeholders, you are building relationships and trust, further developing those vital connections.

Communication is how you get your message out to people. Whether the message is positive or negative, good or bad, practical or impractical—you have a responsibility to ensure you convey that message in the manner you intend. More importantly, you must ensure that you serve the purpose of that communication. In essence, your school's success depends on how effectively you can connect and communicate. Your job involves setting the vision for your school; identifying the strengths and areas for improvement for your school; establishing goals for your school; hiring and retaining top talent for your school; creating a safe and welcoming environment for your school; managing the day-to-day operations of your school; and the list of responsibilities goes on and on. The reality is that you will struggle to fulfill these responsibilities effectively if you are unable to communicate effectively.

As important as it is to ensure you communicate effectively because the day-to-day functions of the work depend on you conveying the message you intend, it is also important to do more. Burnison (2012) states, "For a leader, communication is connection and inspiration—not just transmission of information" (p. 151). Not only is communication essential for conveying information, it is also critical for inspiring and motivating your stakeholders.

Part of your job as a school leader is to inspire and motivate your teachers and others so that they feel supported and encouraged in their unique visions; however, it is also to fulfill your mission and to achieve your goals. As a leader, it is your job to ensure teachers are motivated and inspired to make a positive impact on every student they teach. You, ultimately, are responsible for continuing to articulate and implement the mission and goals, which in turn guide this positive impact. When you communicate, whether it's in a meeting or through the one-on-one conversations you have with your teachers and staff, you should be consistently inspiring them and motivating them so they can be the best they can be for your students. School leaders always have a responsibility to do this for the betterment of their students. Whether it's monitoring expectations or introducing a new policy to improve the school—we can't coerce our staff into doing things. We have to inspire and motivate them through clear and consistent communication.

Take a moment to think about the latest request you made of your staff. Did you ask that teachers collaborate weekly? Or that they review data from their student assessments? Was it that teachers needed to provide effective interventions when students didn't master the standards? Or that they provide enrichment for students who were mastering the standards? Did you ask teachers to follow up with parents within a reasonable amount of time? Or that they rely on effective classroom management skills instead of writing students up for everything? All of these are examples of expectations you may have communicated. When you communicate expectations, you can give directives and hope for the best, or you can truly connect with teachers and other stakeholders by communicating clearly and consistently, fostering trust while inspiring and motivating them to *want* to do the things you ask them to do.

Poor communication can be unclear, but it can also lack empathy for and understanding of the effect it might have on the receiver. Think of the impact this can have. Kevin Murray (2013) states, "Leaders who cannot communicate well, who lack the human touch, can create organizations which are toxic to work in, filled with turmoil and conflict, going nowhere, achieving little" (p. 2). I'm willing to bet that it's possible to trace quite a few troubling issues in your school to ineffective communication. Many conflicts and concerns are rooted in either lack of communication or miscommunication. Teachers not knowing something or parents hearing rumors—issues like these typically stem from poor communication. This can happen frequently during crisis-type situations. Once I had a fire alarm go off, and I was unable to send an email to the community right away. Within minutes, rumors were flying, from "There was a fire in the cafeteria" to "The building collapsed because of the flames" when in actuality, a student had pulled the fire alarm and there was no fire. Richard DuFour and Michael Fullan (2013) sum this up when they say, "The effectiveness of educational systems at all levels is diminished without clear communication from a cohesive team of leaders" (p. 25).

The challenges are complex and varied, but the solutions are surprisingly simple. By mastering the five modes of communication that this book covers, you will have the tools you need to lead your school to success for every student. The next section contains an overview of this book along with descriptions of each of the different types of communication that every leader should be aware of.

About This Book

This book is divided into five chapters. Each chapter discusses a form of verbal, nonverbal, or written communication. You undoubtedly use one or more of these on a daily basis. Each chapter ends with reflection questions to give you an opportunity to process what you have learned and to reflect on your current communication practices to see how you can improve them. In addition, at the end of every chapter, you will find several reproducible pages. The first of these is that chapter's corresponding challenge, which guides you through using the rest of the reproducibles to analyze your strengths and weaknesses, create personal goals to strengthen and reinforce your skills, and put your learning into action.

Chapter 1: Communicating Through Presentations

This chapter begins with outlining all the different purposes presentations serve. I share how to structure presentations along with what elements make presentations effective or ineffective. The chapter also explores ways to be a charismatic presenter and the importance of soliciting quality feedback in order to improve your presentation skills.

Chapter 2: Communicating Through Meetings

In this chapter, I outline the different types of meetings school leaders can have and the different purposes meetings serve. I also share elements of what makes meetings effective or ineffective.

Chapter 3: Communicating Through Tough Conversations

This chapter reviews the different purposes tough conversations serve as well as discussing when those conversations are necessary. I explore barriers that can prevent you from having tough conversations, and share elements of ineffective tough conversations. The chapter ends by providing strategies for effective tough conversations.

Chapter 4: Communicating Through Writing

This chapter goes into the different purposes written communication serves. I explore the various advantages and disadvantages of written communication as well as the different types of written communication. The chapter ends by providing various strategies for effective writing.

Chapter 5: Communicating Through Body Language

This chapter begins with outlining the impact body language has on communication. I explore body language communication as it relates to the face, arms and hands, and legs and feet. The chapter also explores how your appearance and emotional intelligence play a role in body language. The chapter ends by providing tips for leaders on appropriate body language.

The Five-Month Communication Challenge

All five chapters culminate with a segment of a communication challenge that you can use to improve your skills. Each chapter segment pertains to the contents of that specific chapter. That is, the five-month communication challenge consists of five individual challenges that should each last one month.

During each month, follow the suggestions in the challenge column. For example, if you decide to read the book in order, the first chapter is about presentations and the challenge will help you improve your skills in presenting—do that challenge every time you present during that month. When you move on to the next month, continue with those tasks to increase the effectiveness of your presentations, but then add on the next challenge for every meeting you have in the next month. At the end of each month, reflect on the ways in which that challenge impacted your communication. By the end of the fifth month, you should have mastered effective presentations, meetings, tough conversations, writing, and body language.

Time to Take Up the Challenge

As you get ready to learn tips and strategies on how to communicate more effectively in order to lead more effectively, keep in mind you do not need to read the chapters in order. I have designed each chapter in such a way that it stands on its own, so you can go directly to the chapters that you most want information on, and then commit to improve your skills with the corresponding challenge, where you incorporate the tips and strategies outlined in each chapter into your practice. The challenge is a good way to ensure you will put your new learning into practice. Many times, we learn about great things, but we never change our practice so we don't get better. This challenge will help you sharpen your communication skills, so I challenge you to take it!

CHAPTER 1

Communicating Through Presentations

The success of your presentation will be judged not by the knowledge you send but by what the listener receives.

—Lilly Walters

School leaders present all the time to a variety of stakeholders. In fact, leading presentations is almost certainly a common task that you partake in. Presentations to faculty, parents, students, business partners, and others are a regular occurrence in the educational leader's world. Because of how much you present, and how important the messages are, it's essential to ensure that you continually improve your ability to present effectively. "Conveying and selling a poignant, memorable message takes specific knowledge and skills. Do you know them? Do you have them?" (Heflebower, 2019, p. 8). As a result of the frequency and the potential impact, presenting is a critical communication skill— a presentation is your chance as a leader to inspire your stakeholders to do what is best for students. Chris Anderson (2016), curator of TED Talks, uses the phrase *presentation literacy* to say that anyone can learn the skills to present effectively and that, in fact, "In the 21st century, presentation literacy should be taught in every school" (p. 7).

I define presentations in this book as mostly one-way communication when the school leader is standing in the front, communicating to his or her audience for a variety of different purposes. If you're encouraging a lot of participation or dialogue in a presentation, I would consider that more of a meeting than a presentation (see chapter 2, page 35). That being said, this doesn't mean that you do *all* the talking in a presentation. For instance, if you are conducting a presentation, you may include opportunities for the participants to interact with each other or engage in activities—but they are talking with each other.

This chapter first outlines the various purposes of presentations. Then, it describes a variety of different ways to structure presentations. Next, it examines what elements make presentations effective versus ineffective. Lastly, the chapter discusses how school leaders can be charismatic when presenting and how to solicit feedback from participants in an effort to improve.

Purpose of Presentations

As a school leader, you would always expect your teachers to have a clear purpose for every lesson. What exactly should students be able to know or do after that particular lesson? It is the same with presentations. Every presentation has to have a purpose. What should the audience be able to know or do after the presentation is over? In this section, I review the various reasons school leaders make presentations.

Information Sharing

School leaders prepare presentations to share information with their faculty and staff, students, parents, or business partners. Presentations that are designed to share information are powerful because they are your opportunities to communicate vital information that stakeholders need to know. Examples of vital information include the following.

- Strategic plan
- Safety plan
- School procedures and expectations
- Student handbook (expectations for students)
- State of the school address

Although the plans in the preceding list may appear in written form, there are many times when school leaders need to verbally present these plans to the staff in order to reinforce them. In these information-sharing sessions, the leader communicates the information that is written in the plans to ensure everyone understands it. It is in the school leader's best interest to ensure the staff members understand this information, and communicating these plans verbally is important to meeting that goal.

Developing Professionally

Sometimes school leaders prepare presentations to deliver professional development to the faculty, staff, and even parents. These presentations are designed to communicate new knowledge and learning that will help the staff perform better and possibly help the parents support the school more effectively. Examples of topics for professional development presentations include the following.

- Instructional practices
- Grading practices
- How to support students (for parents)
- College preparation (for parents)

Convincing and Influencing

Presentations can convince faculty, staff, parents, or students to do something that involves change. These presentations can be difficult because, through this communication, school leaders are carrying out the ultimate leadership act, which is to influence a group of people to change something. This is not always an easy task—which makes the communication in this type of presentation even more tricky. Examples of reasons why you may need to present to convince or influence audience members include the following.

- New policies
- New master schedule
- Rollout of an initiative or program
- Budget

Motivating

Every now and then, you need to motivate your faculty or students. These presentations are necessary when you can feel that folks are beginning to lose their momentum or enthusiasm—or a big event is occurring that the faculty or students need to get energized for. The communication through these presentations needs to encourage or inspire the audience. Appropriate times for motivational presentations include the following.

- Right before state testing
- Beginning of the school year
- Beginning of a new semester or grading period

Celebrating and Team Building

There are times when school leaders need to celebrate great news, and the best way to deliver it is through a presentation. Or sometimes, the presentation may be to incorporate team-building activities to promote trust and fellowship among the faculty. This communication should always be positive and fun for your teachers and staff. Examples of appropriate occasions for this type of presentation include the following.

- Reaching a goal
- Accomplishment of a milestone
- Recognition of faculty or a team

Just as you would expect teachers to always know the purpose of their lessons each day, you must also know the purpose of any presentation you give. When you are clear on the purpose of your presentation, you can think about what strategies to incorporate to fulfill that purpose.

Structure of Effective Presentations

The first step after figuring out the purpose of the presentation is to create an outline or a structure for it. Creating a structure for your presentation helps organize your thoughts into a clear logical sequence—which then will help the audience follow your presentation better. Doing your presentation without organizing and structuring your content first is like a movie director hiring actors and actresses and filming the movie without having the script first (Atkinson, 2005). Structuring your presentation will also help you remember the presentation as you are communicating the message to your audience.

This section will outline a variety of structures you can use when preparing your presentations.

Chronological Structure

This structure is useful when you need to communicate information based on a time line. It is logical because the communication follows the order of the dates. For example, you can use this structure when sharing data from previous school years all the way up to the current school year. The purpose here is to help your stakeholders understand where you've been and where you currently are. In other words, you can illuminate what your school's reality was and what it is now—and maybe even what you want your reality to look like in the future.

Sequential Structure

You can use this structure when you are communicating information about a certain process, expectation, or procedure that listeners will all need to do in a specific way. A time to use this structure might be when you share specific procedures for how teachers should administer discipline or execute testing schedules. There's a first, then second, then third, then fourth kind of structure to these presentations. The benefit of this structure is that you can arrange the information in order of importance. For example, begin with the most important piece of information that your stakeholders need to hear—or work backward and end with the most important piece of information so your presentation leads up to that part. A leader beginning with the most important piece of information might share information that the staff has been waiting to hear—maybe the results of a survey (for example, the staff voted on implementing schedule A instead of schedule B). After that announcement, the rest of the presentation may be about what this means for the community and how the school will facilitate the change. On the other hand, an example of a presentation where the school leader ends with the most important piece of information could be when he or she is introducing the staff to a new initiative or idea. The buildup of the presentation could be the case for why, with data and examples, and then the school leader would end by communicating that initiative. The point here is that the information should always be communicated in an order that makes sense and is logical.

Advantages and Disadvantages Structure

Whether you are trying to inform or persuade your stakeholders through your presentation, this structure organizes your content into two categories: (1) the advantages of your message and (2) the disadvantages of your message. No matter what information you are communicating, there are usually pros and cons to it. For example, if you are communicating a new policy or a new initiative, you may want to structure your content in this manner. This is also a good structure to use before you make a decision on something, as you let the stakeholders know the pros and cons of each issue before deciding which one to go with.

Problem and Solution Structure

School leaders almost always have a problem to tackle. This structure is perfect for when you are attempting to problem solve in order to improve your school. In this presentation structure, you identify and communicate the problem. Then you present a variety of solutions and help the audience select the best solution. If you have already predetermined the solution, then you describe the problem and communicate the solution. An example could be when the problem has to do with student performance declining in writing. In this case, a school leader might present solutions to help improve writing schoolwide. Or, another problem could be student discipline, and you share solutions to help prevent students from violating school rules. This structure basically divides the presentation into two main parts: (1) the problem and (2) the solutions.

Compare and Contrast Structure

Sometimes you need to juxtapose multiple concepts and, in that case, a compare and contrast structure could help organize the information. When you compare concepts, you are identifying how they are similar, and when you are contrasting concepts, you are identifying how they are different. Communicating information through a compare and contrast method is another way to help your stakeholders organize information logically. An example could be to compare and contrast current students with students from ten years earlier to demonstrate how teaching methods should or should not change. You can also compare and contrast how your school implemented something in the past with how you might implement something in the present to decide what to include in implementation and how best to do it.

Cause and Effect Structure

This structure allows you to present information in a way that demonstrates the effect of something. In other words, what impact has something made? In this structure, you would outline the cause (the *what*) and then describe the effect (the end result). Or you can explain the current situation (the end result) and then explore the causes (the *what*) for that situation. An example could be when a school leader communicates the current reality that it took eight minutes for the entire school to evacuate during a fire drill when in the past it was always done within three minutes. After this message, the school leader can share the reasons that may have led to the eight-minute evacuation.

Elements of Ineffective Presentations

Everyone has sat through an ineffective presentation. Think of an occasion when you were in the audience when someone was presenting and the entire time you thought about everything *but* what the presenter was discussing. In other words, you were not engaged and, therefore, you were not paying attention. If an ineffective presentation means your audience is not very engaged or even paying attention at all, then that means that presentation will most likely fail to meet the purpose you have set for it.

The American Management Association (2015) conducted a survey of 360 people to find out what annoyed them the most in presentations. The results show that the most annoying habit is when the presenter reads the slides (37 percent); second is when the presenter lacks knowledge about what he or she is presenting (22 percent); and third is when the presenter uses too many distracting words such as *um* or *uh* (16 percent).

This section outlines those elements in addition to some others that lead to ineffective presentations. These are the things not to do when preparing and delivering a presentation as a school leader.

Lack of Knowledge

There are times when school leaders have to present topics they may not be familiar with. Maybe this has happened to you: you receive some information from the state or district that you do not know a lot about but are responsible for communicating to your teachers. Or you could be communicating something that is out of your comfort zone or expertise area. When a school leader does not have strong knowledge of the content that he or she is communicating, this can lead to the bad habit of reading off the slides. As a result, the presentation can be ineffective because the audience is not taking it seriously—because listeners can tell the presenter is simply reading off slides and doesn't really don't know what he or she is talking about. Without strong knowledge of the topic, you may struggle to effectively convey your message to the audience.

Lack of Preparation

On the other hand, you may know the topic really, really well. Sometimes a school leader knows a topic and thinks he or she can just present it without preparing for it. No matter how well leaders know a topic or how well they may think they know what they want to accomplish with the presentation, it's essential to spend time preparing for it. Your stakeholders will notice when you deliver a presentation that you have not prepared for. With any projects or tasks that you do, good preparation increases your chances of success. Not preparing can lead to an ineffective presentation because it increases the chances that you will not accomplish your purpose. For example, I remember one instance when I had to do a presentation on one portion of our strategic plan. Now, I knew that strategic plan forward and backward—surely I could present on this with my eyes closed. So I didn't really prepare for the presentation because I thought I could just wing it. When I began presenting, I knew right away it wasn't going well. My message was confusing, and the teachers looked bored. I spoke the entire time, without giving them any time to process or digest the information I was giving them. My purpose with that presentation was to inform the teachers of how we were going to implement a part of our strategic plan, and I know I failed because teachers left that meeting confused. The plan that I wanted to implement did not happen (until I called another meeting for which I was much more prepared). My lack of preparation, despite my familiarity with the subject, completely undermined my message.

Lack of Purpose

When presentations have no purpose, the audience is left asking themselves, "What was the point of that presentation?" Your audience is likely to be full of busy educators who want to feel that you value their time. When there is no purpose, then what exactly is the learning outcome or your desired end result? If you are just communicating without any goal, your presentation will be ineffective because you will have achieved nothing at the end of it. Unfortunately, I see this happen too often in schools and districts. Think about this scenario and see if you have experienced this: chances are, you already have all your staff meetings where you conduct presentations scheduled on your calendar for the year, right? Have you ever experienced a moment where you realize you have a presentation in two days and you have no idea what you're going to say? So, you quickly put some slides together to fill that time up (or have other people come out and talk for you). When your presentation becomes a time filler, you have an ineffective presentation. Every presentation needs to have a purpose, just like we expect teachers to have a purpose for every lesson plan they create.

Off Topic

When you go off topic during a presentation, you risk derailing your message and your purpose for that communication. It can be easy to get off topic sometimes but when that does occur, keep in mind, you are now beginning to make the presentation ineffective. School leaders need to be able to read the audience so they pick up on body language signals such as confused looks or bored facial expressions. The message becomes convoluted as you begin to discuss other items. An easy way to get off topic is when a teacher asks a question or makes a comment while you are presenting. The presentation becomes ineffective because you are no longer communicating about what you were supposed to and therefore you may not fulfill the purpose of the presentation. In addition, sometimes school leaders go off topic because they're trying to say as much as they can during the limited time they have—we all know how hard it is to call faculty meetings before or after school. When you do have the opportunity to hold the attention of the audience, it's important to resist the urge to cram in as much information as possible, which can take away from the real purpose of that presentation. This is why it is important to have a plan for your presentation, because if you stick to your plan, you are less likely to go off topic.

The Delivery

One major reason that presentations can be ineffective is their delivery. The way school leaders communicate information can make the presentation ineffective because the audience may not be able to pay attention or understand. There are several presentation delivery missteps school leaders can make. First, sometimes school leaders, in an effort to appear as intelligent and knowledgeable as possible, will use vocabulary that consists of jargon that the audience may not understand. Another problem is the use of distractors, such as too many *um*s, *uh*s, and *like*s. These distractors draw audience attention away from the message. Sometimes, the presenter is simply boring, often when the school leader's voice and tone are monotonous and lack energy and enthusiasm. A boring presentation is an ineffective one because the audience has to work too hard to stay engaged.

Use of PowerPoint

When looking at the elements of ineffective presentations, we need to discuss the use of PowerPoint and other presentation software. Presentation programs that rely on digital slides, especially PowerPoint, have become a common tool that school leaders use to help deliver presentations, but they can sometimes become the most ineffective element. Here's how.

Too Much Text

One common mistake is to put too much text on each slide, making it difficult for the audience to read. When school leaders try to cram too much text onto each slide, that means the font is probably too small for audience members to read comfortably. Whatever you do, *never* read word for word from the slides.

Too Many Animations and Sounds

In an attempt to be fun and engaging, school leaders may go overboard with sound effects and animation. Too many of these kinds of effects can be distracting and therefore ineffective. Remember—the audience will be reading from left to right, so using animations that are counter to that increases the likelihood of distraction.

Distracting Backgrounds and Color

When using PowerPoint for a presentation, school leaders need to choose a background and color for their slides. That choice can sometimes lead to an ineffective presentation because the background might distract the audience or make the content hard to read. This is where you need to carefully select your backgrounds and colors for your slides so they are not too bright or busy. It helps to create a schoolwide template with your school colors and logo that everyone can use consistently when delivering presentations.

No Clicker

Using a PowerPoint without a clicker can be distracting. When someone else has to advance your slides when you either say "Next" or nod to indicate it's time for the next slide, it takes away from your actual presentation. Controlling this yourself gives audience members a far more seamless experience.

Handouts

When the audience receives PowerPoint as a handout, the presentation can become ineffective. Participants end up reading the slides and become distracted as the focus is on reading instead of listening to you. Jerry Weissman (2004) says that "a presentation is a presentation and only a presentation, and never a document" (p. 103). Handouts of the slides also minimize the importance of the actual presentation as teachers may think if they just get the copy of the slides, they won't miss much by not being in attendance for the actual presentation. Therefore, your handouts should not be the actual slides but rather provide important takeaway information, which could include a graphic organizer that the audience fills out as you're speaking or a summary page with the key points.

Elements of Effective Presentations

Now that you know what can make your presentation ineffective, this section reviews several strategies and tips to help you make your presentation effective.

Clear Beginning, Middle, and End

Every effective presentation has a clear beginning, middle, and end. This requires school leaders to spend time knowing and understanding what the purpose of the presentation is and then prepare an outline for how the presentation will begin, what the content in the middle of the presentation will be, and how the presentation will end. Not only is this good for making your presentations effective, it is also a good way to model good teaching practices. Every time school leaders present is an opportunity to demonstrate what good teaching should look like.

The beginning of the presentation is where you capture the attention of your audience. For every presentation you create and deliver, think through how you will start it. There are many great strategies for opening your presentation. As teachers and other staff are walking in, you can play music and have a slide up with an opener such as a quote that they need to reflect on or an open-ended question related to the presentation that they can answer or discuss with their colleagues. Starting with a thought-provoking task (that is related to your presentation) such as answering an open-ended question or thinking about a quote engages the audience right away. You are putting your listeners in the right frame of mind for your presentation. Another engaging strategy for opening your presentation is to start with a story (again, a story that is related to your presentation). You can also begin with a *what if* or *imagine* scenario in which you ask your audience to think about a particular concept or situation related to your presentation. Weissman (2004) shares the following suggestions for opening a presentation.

- Factoid (share a surprising statistic or a little-known fact)
- Retrospective or prospective (take a look backward or forward)
- Aphorism (use a familiar saying)

The middle of the presentation needs to contain two main points: (1) content and (2) execution of that content. You should structure it in such a way that the content is organized and makes sense, and the audience can follow it. Eric Garner (2012) quotes American businessman Phil Crosby who states, "No one can remember more than three points." You should limit the number of main ideas or key points you communicate in your presentation to three or fewer so that the audience learns or remembers them. Inundating people with too much information during a presentation isn't always a good idea. Imagine sitting in a one-hour presentation where the presenter talks about the following items.

- New school board policy on grading
- Expectations for safety procedures
- New bus transportation changes
- Requirements for the annual evaluation instrument
- Student discipline hearing procedures

All those topics covered in one hour? Your mind will want to explode. And quite honestly, at some point, it will become difficult to continue to pay attention because of the sheer volume of information coming your way. Now of course all these topics are important, but think about how to effectively plan to deliver information so that you're not communicating everything all at once. Instead, aim for manageable chunks.

The second aspect that you should plan for is how you deliver that content. What instructional strategies will you use throughout the presentation to keep the audience engaged? Before examining those kinds of strategies, it is important to note the average attention span of adults. Several authors have stated that the average amount of

time an adult audience member can pay attention is twenty minutes (Goodman &
Cause Communications, 2006; Rehn, 2016). This means that after twenty minutes
or so, the audience begins to stop listening, gets bored, or thinks of other things
unrelated to the presentation. Molecular biologist John Medina (2008) supports the
ten-minute rule. In other words, after about ten minutes, the brain just becomes
uninterested. Based on this research, an effective presentation includes something
every ten to twenty minutes to get the audience either up and moving or talking in
groups. No staff member wants to listen to school leaders talk for more than ten to
twenty minutes at a time, so build certain strategies into your presentation that take
this into consideration. Those strategies can include the following.

- Turn and talk to a neighbor about a specific question.

- Use chart paper to brainstorm ideas.

- Role-play a situation or scenario.

- View short video clips.

- Have participants express their viewpoint by physically going to a certain part
  of the room (body voting).

- Utilize case studies to reflect on a problem or issue.

As you may have noticed, all these strategies require the audience to interact.
Presentations should never be a sit and get—you want to build time in for the audience members to engage so they can learn and process the information you have
given them. Again, a good rule of thumb is to incorporate an engaging, interactive
activity after about ten to twenty minutes of speaking. This means, if your presentation is about an hour long, you should build in at least three to four interactive
activities throughout to keep your faculty and staff involved. Be sure to use a variety
of strategies in your presentations so you don't become predictable. If you keep using
the same strategies every time you present, you may lose impact. The reproducible
"Interactive Strategies for Presentations" (page 30) provides a menu of interactive
strategies that you can use in your presentations to get your audience to interact with
each other to stay engaged.

After a strong opening and great middle, you must plan out how you will close the
presentation. How will it end? In their book *Why Bad Presentations Happen to Good
Causes*, Andy Goodman and Cause Communications (2006) talk about the particular
importance of the beginning and the end of presentations. They explain that it is at
these two points that the attention of the audience is at its peak:

> It's human nature. When we first sit down, we are curious
> about the . . . subject . . . and when we hear the words "In
> conclusion," even those among us in the deepest reaches of
> REM sleep will awaken and look to the podium, awaiting those

words of wisdom that make it all worthwhile. (Goodman &
Cause Communications, 2006, p. 32)

Since the end of the presentation is your time to reiterate the main purpose of your presentation, you want to do it well because the audience is most likely listening. The reproducible "Presentation Preparation Outline" (page 29) is a template that you can use to plan out your presentation beginning, middle, and end.

A public question-and-answer session is usually not a good way to end a presentation in the school environment because it opens up the floor for off-topic questions or for questions that steer people away from your original purpose. For example, if the purpose of the presentation was to provide information about a new initiative coming up, you may get questions such as "We tried this five years ago, and it didn't work—so what if it doesn't work again?" Or you may get inundated with *what if* questions. Although a presentation is when you as the school leader are imparting information to the audience for a specific purpose, there are many ways to gather input and feedback from the audience without derailing that purpose. You can bring index cards for the audience members to write their questions on, which they can submit to you as they walk out the door. Or make yourself available at the end of the presentation for one-to-one questions. Another possibility is to post chart paper on a wall, and participants can write their questions there that you can address after the presentation, either in person or via an online platform. If the situation calls for it, you can even conduct meetings with smaller groups of people prior to or after the presentation to reinforce the same purpose and make sure that everyone feels heard and supported (see chapter 2, page 35).

You also do not want to end the presentation by making announcements completely unrelated to the presentation. For example, if your presentation was a professional development session on classroom management skills, don't end with something like "Remember to turn your grades in by Friday." When school leaders end their carefully honed presentations with unrelated announcements, it takes away from the message of the presentation because now teachers walk away only remembering those announcements.

Another closing strategy that I do not recommend is asking an open-ended question that invites unrelated contributions from the audience. For example, a school leader might ask the audience, "Does anyone have anything for the group?" or "Any announcements for the good of the group?" Again, doing this risks losing the message of the presentation because the audience is going to walk out thinking about something other than the topic of the presentation. If you delivered a very effective presentation, hopefully there is good energy in the room. When you open the floor up for off-topic comments, it's likely that energy will dissipate before people leave rather than staying with them. Be in control of your ending. End the presentation with a summary or recap of your main purpose. The summary could include next steps for what you expect the teachers to do after the presentation. Using an exit ticket activity, such as a question on a sheet of paper, a sticky note, or even an online app, that participants turn in is not only a good way to engage your participants and summarize your presentation but another way to model good teaching practices for your teachers.

Preparation

Now that you have seen the importance of putting a presentation together with a clear beginning, middle, and end, it's time to see that good preparation is also critical to an effective presentation. Preparation begins with the purpose. What is the point of the presentation? Once you know your purpose, then begin thinking about the *how*. How are you going to meet that purpose? This is where I encourage brainstorming. Think about all the content that you need to share to meet the purpose of the presentation. Write all that content down—either on index cards or type it up. Weissman (2004) shares the importance of a data dump during the brainstorming phase. *Data dump* is the "shapeless outpouring of everything the presenter knows about the topic" (Weissman, 2004, p. 38). Ineffective presentations throw all this information at the audience. But in effective presentations, the presenter does the brain dump during the brainstorming phase. This is where you put everything you think is relevant down on paper. Then, you can "sort, select, eliminate, add and organize these raw materials into a form that flows logically and compellingly from Point A to Point B" (Weissman, 2004, p. 22). Organizing all this content is essential to ensuring the presentation makes sense to the audience. One of the best ways to organize your thoughts from your brainstorming session is to group them by similar themes. For example, write your ideas down on sticky notes, put them up on a wall, and group them according to similarities and differences—these become your big ideas. Or use an electronic platform to create a graphic organizer to group and chunk your thoughts into themes. Use whatever method works for you as long as it helps to organize your ideas.

Once you have prepared your content, think through what visual aids or handouts you may need. Visual aids and handouts should help reinforce the purpose of your presentation by helping the audience process what you are communicating. Always provide handouts that you need the audience to reference or work on (maybe during an engaging activity) but not in the beginning. Otherwise, you lose people's attention as the audience begins reading the handouts instead of paying attention to what you have to say.

You also have to prepare the room where you will be presenting. Many school leaders present in places such as the media center, theater, cafeteria, classroom, or other space in the school designated for gatherings. Think about how you want the room to be laid out and whether you need to arrange anything in advance. Do you want the audience sitting in rows or at tables in groups?

Dress

Even though your staff probably sees you every day and is aware of your sense of style, before a presentation, take the time to plan out your wardrobe. When you are standing in front of your faculty and staff, addressing them with an important message, you must be dressed professionally. Avoid colors that are too loud, such as bright pink or red. You want the attention to be on the content of the presentation—not you. Black, navy, and gray are safe, conservative, professional colors to wear.

Ensure the outfits you wear on the days you present fit you well and make you feel confident. Clean and iron them so they are wrinkle free. You want to walk in there with a sense of authority, confidence, and command of the material you are about to present; pick an outfit that makes you feel that way.

Remember that when you are standing in front of your faculty and staff, they are looking at you. Human nature is to observe your appearance. Carefully think through your outfit, including your shoes. Ensure your shoes are clean and in good condition. Consider your accessories and make sure they're not overkill. In addition, ensure what you are wearing is conservative (for example, appropriate fit and so on). The last thing to remember is your hair. Keep it neat and clean, including facial hair.

PowerPoint

I explained earlier how PowerPoint can lead to ineffective presentations. However, slides that accompany your presentation can be a benefit as long as you keep in mind that their purpose is to help the audience better understand your message. The slides are not for the presenter. With that said, how can slides be a visual tool to enhance your presentation and help you meet your purpose?

Presentation Template

All school leaders should create a presentation template with their school colors and maybe even the school's mission or mascot. Most companies and businesses use custom templates for their own internal presentations. This prevents one having to pick from already created templates that may be too distracting with their fonts or color choices. Creating a presentation template for your school gives your presentations a professional and polished look.

The Text

You can present your text in one of two ways: either (1) in bullets or (2) in sentences (Weissman, 2009). Think of bullets as headlines or major topics—the audience sees each one as you speak about it. Use sentences only to make a certain point—otherwise you run the risk of losing the audience as people begin reading the sentences while at the same time trying to listen to you. The 4 × 4 rule is a useful guideline for your slides—four lines with four words on each line (Weissman, 2004).

Legibility

Use fonts that are easy to read. Illiya Vjestica (2012) recommends five fonts for presentations.

1. Helvetica (neutral and simple)
2. Garamond (mature and professional)
3. Futura (elegant and understated)
4. Gill Sans (warm and friendly)
5. Rockwell (powerful and bold)

This is not the time to be creative; the font should be simple and legible. In addition, the font size should be big enough that the people in the very back can read it. When putting bullets up, ensure there are about four bullets on each slide. This will not only help with legibility (because there is less text on the slide, it will make the words big enough to read easily) but also keep the focus on your message.

One Bullet at a Time

Ensure that each point appears on the screen as you talk about it (instead of having the slide come up with all the points). In other words, the only thing on the screen should be what you are talking about at that time. As you hit *next* with the clicker, the next point should come up that you are now about to discuss. I recommend the basic *appear* option instead of the others such as *spin, dissolve in,* or *blinds*. These are showy but can detract from your message. To most effectively meet your purpose, it is best to keep any kind of movement on the slides conservative to keep your audience's attention on the message you are communicating.

Graphics

Graphics can be a great way to explain or show a specific concept. They can be your own pictures you have taken to show something. For example, you might share a picture of a classroom to show how you want teachers to organize their classrooms. Or, graphics could be pictures you find online to show examples of the concept you are talking about. Visual images are a great way to use PowerPoint slides as they demonstrate and enhance your message. Another benefit of adding graphics is that they are not text, which means you must talk to your audience without ever reading anything. Some public speakers use *only* graphics on their slides—try that one time for your presentation.

Charisma

When considering charisma, think about all the words that are considered synonyms.

- Charm
- Appeal
- Magnetism
- Allure
- Attractiveness
- Captivation

Keeping these words in mind, if you think about a charismatic person, who comes to mind? Why? What makes this person charismatic? In this section, I argue that charisma is something you can learn. With practice, any school leader can be charismatic. If you can improve your skills in this area, you increase the likelihood that your presentations will be effective because your faculty is more likely to listen and pay attention to your message. Public speaker and executive coach Olivia Fox Cabane (2012) says, "Charisma gets people to like you, trust you, and want to be led by you" (p. 2).

To learn to be charismatic, first, be confident. It is so easy to spot when people are insecure or unsure of themselves, and if someone is unsure of him- or herself, others become unsure of that person. Know your material and deliver it with authority and assertiveness. Be positive and believe in your ability, experiences, skills, and knowledge—nobody can do this for you. Having self-confidence is key to being a charismatic presenter.

Charismatic presenters always bring energy into their presentations, but for some school leaders, this may be difficult to do. International authority on personal presence Achim Nowak (2004) states that bringing energy into a presentation doesn't feel natural to some—but being "low-key and restrained does" (p. 56). Many of us in school leadership positions have grown into being reserved and calm in order to connect with teachers, parents, or students in numerous one-to-one interactions. But when presenting, you have the opportunity to connect in a different way by becoming the focal point of everyone's attention. When you incorporate energy into your presentation, it says, "I value you as an audience member. I take you seriously. I don't wish to bore you. No, my intent is to engage, excite, stimulate, and motivate you" (p. 58).

Use an enthusiastic tone of voice (which doesn't necessarily mean speaking loudly; it just means to infuse some passion into your message). Show that you are excited about your topic and audience, and believe in it. Use words that convey that enthusiasm such as those Steve Jobs would often use: *unbelievable, awesome, cool,* and *huge* (Gallo, 2017). In addition, change the tone of your voice to keep the audience engaged. For certain points, you may need to soften your voice, and for other points, you may need to increase your pitch. Or sometimes you may need to lower or raise the volume of your voice again, depending on the message. The main point here is that the tone and volume of your voice cannot be monotone. There needs to be some enthusiasm as well as variation of your voice throughout the presentation.

Think about an ineffective presentation that you sat through; chances are you can think of one that was ineffective because it was boring. Reflect on what made it boring. Was it the presenter? If you dig even further, you may conclude that it was boring because of the way the presenter spoke. There are times when school leaders have such important information to share, but the audience members are not engaged and therefore may not even be listening—all because the presenter has lulled them into this state with a monotone voice. The presentation could be organized very well and have all the right components—but could still fall flat because of the delivery.

Be conscientious of your facial expressions as well as the gestures you make while presenting. Your audience will have a tendency to copy your facial expressions—think about how when you smile and nod, people in the audience will sometimes do the same. So, remember to smile during your presentation! In addition, some gestures will distract the audience (such as swaying back and forth or putting your hands in your pockets). In fact, Cabane (2012) uses James Bond as an example, saying we can never imagine him ever fidgeting as he is always so calm, cool, and collected: "This kind of high-status, high-confidence body language is characterized by how few movements are made" (p. 160). However, every now and then, gestures such as moving your hands with excitement can exude the passion that you want to express (chapter 5, page 113, discusses body language in more detail). The key here is to find the right balance.

Stand when presenting. Sometimes school leaders may choose to sit down in a chair in front of their faculty and staff in an attempt to talk to them on a more personal level—but presenting is presenting. Standing in front of your staff enhances your stage presence and can, in fact, strengthen your charisma. While standing, think about your posture. Stand without anything (for example, a podium) between you and the audience and move about freely to show you are comfortable being up there.

Practice! "Know what you're going to say, when you're going to say it, and how you're going to say it" (Gallo, 2017, p. 193). Practice your presentation as much as possible. And record yourself while practicing so you can make sure you're following all the tips in this chapter. Use the reproducible "Self-Assessment Checklist" (page 32) to self-assess your presentation while you view your recording. Do you appear confident? What are your facial expressions like? Your gestures? Do you have any annoying habits (such as saying *um* or flicking your hair)?

Use occasional personal stories to help the audience stay engaged. A funny or touching anecdote is a great way to get the audience to connect with you and relate to you. Being drawn to stories is a very human trait, and storytelling makes us feel connected to one another: "We're born to love stories. They are instant generators of interest, empathy, emotion, and intrigue" (Anderson, 2016, p. 59). Be sure to relate the story to your content (random stories can take away from your message and leave the audience wondering what your point was). Once you have told the story, always relate it back to the point you were making. Anderson (2016) gives the following tips for storytelling.

- Ensure you know why you're telling the story.
- The goal of the story is to give—to let the audience walk away with either insights, actionable information, perspective, context, or hope.
- The story has to be true.
- Edit out the details that are not necessary to make your point.

When you speak, your audience members will be drawn to you if you are able to build a connection with them. Anderson (2016) talks about the importance of connecting with your audience so that people will give you their minds because "knowledge can't be pushed into a brain. It has to be pulled in" (p. 47). Some suggestions he provides are to make eye contact right from the beginning; show your vulnerability; use humor; get rid of your ego; and, of course, tell stories.

Whenever you are presenting, remember that it is a performance—think about the entertainment industry (Cabane, 2012). Think about how actors and actresses deliver certain enduring performances; what tools do they use to enhance their words? If you google some of the top movie speeches, you may see the following clips.

- *Dead Poets Society*: "Seize the Day" (https://bit.ly/2Y3XFqj)
- *Gladiator*: "My Name Is Maximus" (https://bit.ly/2ovKFIF)
- *Rocky Balboa*: "How Hard You Can Get Hit" (https://bit.ly/1Me9cXL)
- *Miracle*: "Pre-Game" (https://bit.ly/1e0FPqP)
- *Coach Carter*: "Our Deepest Fear" (https://bit.ly/1WwBb9j)

When looking at how the actors perform, watch how they speak. From their enthusiasm, to their passion, to their facial expressions, to their voices—how do they put it all together to make their delivery as charismatic as they do?

Feedback

In *Presenting Perfected: Feedback, Tips, Tricks, and Troubleshooting*, Tammy Heflebower (2019) discusses the value in gaining feedback from your participants after your presentation. She highlights the following criteria for obtaining quality feedback.

- Specific
- Timely
- Right amount
- Focused

Part of your job as a school leader is to always solicit feedback—maybe you have put out surveys or used other methods to ask for feedback and input on your school. Soliciting feedback is a great way to gain information on your presentation skills so that you as a leader can improve. When you present, you don't necessarily know how the experience was for your audience. You don't need to solicit feedback after every presentation, but it's useful to do so maybe once or twice a year. Gathering feedback offers more chances to connect with your staff, parents, and students. Think about this as a strategy to show you are open and willing to improve yourself to be a better communicator and, therefore, a better school leader.

Following are some sample questions you can ask your participants when requesting feedback.

- "What did you enjoy the most about this presentation?"
- "How could I have presented differently to make it better?"
- "Do you have any other feedback or suggestions?"

Summary

Presenting is a performance. School leaders typically present so much that it may be easy to forget how powerful that experience can be for both the audience and the presenter. Presenting is an incredibly influential way to communicate with your faculty and staff, so ensure that you invest the appropriate time and energy in preparing and practicing for every presentation. It is during presentations that you are able to influence your faculty and staff as a group into doing something different or teach them all something new. You can see whatever vision or idea you have in your mind heard and executed by all. Therefore, ~~it is crucial to your leadership to appropriately plan and practice to help you deliver effective, successful presentations.~~

Reflection Questions

1. Reflect on the last presentation you made to an audience. How could you have improved it?

2. Think about the next presentation that you are preparing for. What elements will you now include in order to make it more effective?

3. Part of storytelling is remembering your experiences in order to provide enough facts and details for a good narrative. Journal or summarize three experiences you've had in the last two years that would make good stories. You never know how or when you may use them in a presentation, so it's a good idea to start writing them down as they happen.

4. Part of charisma is being confident. Being confident includes knowing your strengths. What are your top ten strengths? What are you most proud of? What unique skills do you bring to your school leadership team?

The School Leader's Communication Challenge: Presentations

The following challenge is designed to be flexible. Depending on your needs and upcoming schedule, you can pick one presentation that you plan to give this month and follow each step closely, or you can use the provided resources to help you reflect on all of your presentations this month.

Challenge	Notes
• Create a template for your school and use it. • Use the "Presentation Preparation Outline" (page 29) to plan for an engaging opener, middle, and conclusion. • Plan for at least one interactive activity (from the reproducible "Interactive Strategies for Presentations" [page 30]) in the middle of the presentation. • End with an exit ticket. • Record yourself presenting and then complete the self-reflection on the reproducible "Self-Assessment Checklist" (page 32). • Conduct the SWOT analysis (page 33) and monitor your goal.	

Presentation Preparation Outline

Beginning	Middle	End
Hook:	Interactive strategies (to avoid the sit and get for more than ten to twenty minutes):	Conclusion:

Interactive Strategies for Presentations

Strategy	Description
Partner Teach	Participants pair up, and each partner tells the other the one main thing he or she learned during the presentation.
Learning Commitment	Participants make a commitment to their team to change one thing after their new learning from the presentation.
Jigsaw	Participants read a part of a passage or chapter of a book and become "experts" on it. Each participant then shares a summary of his or her passage or chapter so everyone understands the entire book.
Text Summary	Participants text each other summaries of their learning.
Learning Stations	Set up different stations so participants rotate through each one. For example, each learning station could be specific to a topic on grading. At each station, participants do an activity such as reading a passage about the topic and responding on chart paper. As participants rotate through, they continue to add their responses to the chart paper.
Solving Problems	Each participant has a piece of paper where he or she brainstorms a solution to a particular problem—then everybody passes the sheets clockwise, and participants read what someone else wrote and add to it. The group does this three to four times. Together as a large group, participants review all the solutions that the group proposed.
One-Minute Write	Participants have one minute to write about the presentation (what they learned, what they will change, and so on).
Quote Walk	Place a variety of quotes (related to the topic of your presentation) throughout the room and have participants walk around and read each one. Ask them to stand by the one that resonates with them the most. In their groups by the quote, discuss why it resonated with them (each group should discuss among themselves and then, if time permits, the leader can hold a whole-group discussion).

Connecting Through Leadership © 2020 Solution Tree Press • SolutionTree.com
Visit **go.SolutionTree.com/leadership** to download this free reproducible.

Strategy	Description
Debate	Participants get into groups of four to six and number themselves off. Even numbers argue for a particular concept while odd numbers argue against the concept.
Speed Sharing	Each participant is seated in front of another participant. Pairs have thirty seconds to tell each other something about their responses to the presentation (things like what they are most excited to learn, what they did learn, what they will now change as a result of the learning, and so on) or to answer a question from the presentation.

Connecting Through Leadership © 2020 Solution Tree Press • SolutionTree.com
Visit **go.SolutionTree.com/leadership** to download this free reproducible.

Self-Assessment Checklist

	Yes	No	Comments
Do I appear confident?			
Am I energetic?			
Am I telling a story effectively?			
Do I have an enthusiastic voice tone?			
Do I vary the volume of my voice?			
Do I use positive facial expressions?			
Are my gestures annoying?			
Do I demonstrate good posture?			

Connecting Through Leadership © 2020 Solution Tree Press • SolutionTree.com
Visit **go.SolutionTree.com/leadership** to download this free reproducible.

SWOT Analysis on My Presentation Skills

Strengths	Weaknesses	Opportunities	Threats
What are you good at when it comes to presenting?	When presenting, what would you consider your weaknesses?	How can you get better at presenting so that your audience listens, is motivated by you to take action, or is persuaded by you to do something? In other words, how can you present so you meet your purpose every time?	Think of the unforeseen things that can happen (and have happened) during your presentations. How can you prepare for them?

My goal for future presentations:

Connecting Through Leadership © 2020 Solution Tree Press • SolutionTree.com
Visit go.SolutionTree.com/leadership to download this free reproducible.

CHAPTER 2
Communicating Through Meetings

If you had to identify, in one word, the reason why the human race has not achieved, and never will achieve, its full potential, that word would be "meetings."
—Dave Barry

Meetings are an almost daily part of a school leader's routine. Whether it's a quick meeting or a planned hour-long meeting—knowing how to communicate effectively in meetings is vital to ensuring that you reach the outcomes you desire. Michael Mankins, Chris Brahm, and Greg Caimi (2014) find that on average, senior executives spend more than two full days in meetings per week. In fact, businessman and investor Andy Kessler (2015) estimates that there are about eleven million meetings held every day in the United States. Think about how many times in just one day you sit down with someone or a group of people to have a meeting. Starting on a Monday, fill out the chart in figure 2.1 (page 36) to count the hours you spend either facilitating or sitting in a meeting for the entire week. At the end of the five days, total up the number of hours and see how it relates to the average cited by Mankins et al. (2014).

	Monday	Tuesday	Wednesday	Thursday	Friday	Total
Number of Hours Spent in Meetings						

Figure 2.1: How much time do you spend in meetings every week?

Visit **go.SolutionTree.com/leadership** for a free reproducible version of this figure.

How many hours do you spend communicating in meetings? It is essential to ensure that you spend that time wisely and effectively.

In addition, think about your teachers and staff. They attend your meetings—how do they feel after they walk out? Alexandra Luong and Steven G. Rogelberg (2005) conducted a study in which they asked the participants to keep a five-day journal recording how many meetings they attended during that time, how long the meetings were, and their feelings of well-being for each day. Their findings indicate that the more meetings participants attend, the more fatigued they feel. Based on their literature review, Luong and Rogelberg (2005) hypothesize that meetings prevent people from completing certain tasks and give them new information to process—and as a result, participants feel fatigued and overloaded. As a school leader, you must ensure that when you meet with your staff, they do not leave your meetings feeling fatigued or overwhelmed with their work.

For the purpose of this book, I define a *meeting* as an occasion when the school leader is engaging in two-way communication with one or more people during a set amount of time. This is different than a presentation because in a presentation the communication is one-way. Sometimes, you might take the information you learn or gather from meetings and deliver it in a presentation to a larger audience.

This chapter outlines the various types of meetings and the purpose of meetings. I describe elements of ineffective meetings and outline the behaviors that can make them ineffective. I offer suggestions for what you can do to help minimize those behaviors. Finally, I discuss elements of effective meetings.

Types of Meetings

There are two main types of meetings that you can use to communicate with stakeholders: (1) formal and (2) informal.

Formal Meetings

School leaders lead all kinds of formal meetings; some are large-group meetings while others are small-group or perhaps even individual meetings, which are between two people. Formal meetings are preplanned. They are usually on the school calendar, and they recur (maybe once a month or every week). One example of a formal meeting is the school administration meeting, when the entire administrative staff comes together. Another example is the school leadership team meeting, when you see people on staff in leadership roles, such as teacher leaders or administrators. Regular meetings with groups of teachers or staff members in a particular grade level, content area, or department also fall under this category. Parent-teacher association (PTA) and local school council meetings, where you meet with parent and community leaders, are still other examples of formal meetings.

Informal Meetings

Informal meetings are those that come up throughout the school year, the ones that you often schedule without much notice. Typically, these can occur at any time and any place. They could include a meeting with a small group of people about a particular issue, or a quick check-in meeting with an individual. Either way, informal meetings usually take place with a small group of people or an individual, and you can hold them anywhere—in the hallway, in a classroom, in the cafeteria, and so on—without much (or any) advance planning.

Those meetings that you probably know as faculty meetings or staff meetings do not appear in this chapter on purpose. Most often, in these meetings, the entire faculty and staff come together for what purpose? Typically, it is to disseminate information. By definition, this becomes a presentation, not a meeting, because it is not two-way communication.

Purpose of Meetings

With how often school leaders meet, it is important to note that any two meetings on any given day may have completely different purposes. This section outlines these possible purposes. The reason it is so important to know your purpose for calling certain meetings is so you can then fulfill that purpose. Leigh Espy (2017) suggests you ask yourself the following questions before sending out invites for a meeting.

- "Are we meeting simply because it's time for a regularly scheduled meeting?"
- "Are we brainstorming to generate ideas?"
- "Do we need a decision?"
- "Are we working on something that needs to have a concrete outcome (such as a process for something)?"

In the following sections, you'll find some reasons why school leaders have meetings. As you read through them, think about whether every meeting you call fits into one of these reasons. When moving forward with planning meetings, think through your reason for calling each meeting.

Seeking Input

When you hold a meeting for the purpose of seeking input, you are facilitating an opportunity to ask stakeholders for their opinions on something. Your goal during this kind of meeting is to receive their feedback. By the end of this meeting, you should have gathered the input you need to make whatever decision you need to make, thus fulfilling your purpose.

Decision Making

In these kinds of meetings, your purpose is to make a decision with the group. You can discuss a variety of solutions in this meeting and then select one as a group. Or you could explore several options and debate before coming to an agreement on which option to go with. Either way, the purpose of the two-way communication in this meeting is to hold a discussion with the result of making a decision.

Brainstorming

Sometimes you might call meetings for the purpose of sharing different ideas or thoughts. During this kind of a meeting, you lead a discussion to gain as many different ideas as possible for a specific reason. By the end of this meeting, your goal is to have a plethora of suggestions on a particular topic.

Resolving Conflict

You would hold this kind of meeting to resolve a conflict with the members present in the meeting. This could be a group of teachers who are having issues with one another, it could be with a parent who is upset with the school, it could be between two students who continue to have arguments with each other, and so on. The purpose of these meetings is to resolve the conflict and come to an understanding, so the issues do not continue after the meeting is over.

Information Exchanging

Sometimes you might call a meeting with a group of people to have them share various kinds of information with one another. For example, a group of teachers may share information about a specific student. The purpose of these meetings is to educate everyone in the group about a situation so they can be more informed.

Team Building

There are times when you just need to hold a meeting for team-building purposes—that is, to strengthen the team, strengthen trust, and strengthen the rapport among the members. The purpose of this meeting is that, by the end of it, the group comes out a little stronger and little closer together as a team.

Completing Tasks

These meetings occur to give a group of people the opportunity to get together to perform a task. In this meeting, the group gathers to accomplish a project. For example, a team would hold this type of meeting to create testing schedules or open house packets.

You must be clear on the purpose of all your meetings before calling the meetings. As I mentioned in the previous chapter, knowing your purpose is vital to success. In this case, knowing what you want to achieve by the end of the meeting helps you to achieve it. View the purpose of every meeting as a guide to your essential question. What exactly should everyone achieve by the end of your time together? By the end of the meeting, reflect on your purpose or ask questions to see if you achieved your outcome.

Elements of Ineffective Meetings

There is no doubt that with the number of meetings the typical school leader leads, some meetings can be ineffective. The *Harvard Business Review* published an article quantifying this issue. After surveying almost two hundred people in senior management positions, researchers find that 65 percent say meetings keep them from doing their own work and 71 percent say meetings are unproductive and inefficient (Perlow, Hadley, & Eun, 2017).

Think about one of the worst meetings you ever sat in on. What made it so bad? Let's review the possible reasons why some meetings can be ineffective so that as a school leader you can minimize (hopefully eliminate) ineffective meetings that you facilitate in your school.

Too Many People

One mistake that school leaders sometimes make is inviting people to meetings who needn't attend. In an attempt to be inclusive, they don't think through who really needs to be in the meeting. Too many people in a meeting makes it difficult to have efficient and successful two-way communication and therefore get anything accomplished. In fact, Sebastian Bailey (2013) states that "productivity goes down with more meeting attendees." Remember that you hold meetings to have two-way communication for a specific purpose. You can hinder that communication when there are too many people in the room.

The Wrong People

Another issue that comes of trying to be too inclusive is when school leaders invite the wrong people to the meeting. This can create a lot of unwanted outcomes. First, the meeting is ineffective for those people because they may not understand why they are there, and they may feel they are wasting their time. Second, you may receive information you do not really need. For example, if the meeting you called is to seek input on why co-taught classes are not utilizing effective co-teaching strategies, then it may not be a productive discussion if you invite teachers or other staff members who are not in those situations, because their perspectives, while important, have no bearing on the current topic.

Lack of Preparation

As with anything, if you're unprepared, chances are the meeting will not go well. This can manifest in a variety of ways. First, perhaps you just didn't prepare for the content of the meeting. Many busy school leaders have probably ended up in this situation. You know you must meet with a group for a specific purpose, but you're figuring out what you're going to say and do just a few minutes before the meeting is supposed to begin. Another way that you might not prepare is by not bringing the materials that you need for the meeting—maybe handouts or chart paper. These kinds of things are common sense, but when your day is full of meetings and other obligations, it's easy to overlook them. Unpreparedness will always increase the chances of your meeting being ineffective because its planning didn't receive the time and effort necessary to ensure the purpose was fulfilled.

Too Much Information

School leaders understandably fall victim to this often. With so much to go over and never enough time, it's natural to try to jam it all into one meeting. But when a leader tries to bring up as much as possible, the meeting quickly loses its focus— your brain can only handle a few things at one time. Think about a meeting with the school leadership team where the forty-five-minute meeting agenda looks like this.

- Review state test scores (that just got published).
- Discuss open house procedures.
- Change the grading policy.
- Review strategic plan.

Each of these topics is big! In a forty-five-minute meeting, how effective will be the discussion and, more importantly, the outcomes? Before the meeting even begins, you can be certain it has a high chance of being ineffective because there is just too much on the agenda and, therefore, no clear purpose or outcome.

Lack of Focus

Like any school leader, you likely have a lot on your plate. Multitasking is your norm. You are probably used to constantly doing a variety of tasks at the same time, including responding to emails and texts from various people while juggling other obligations like facilitating a meeting. When you are leading a meeting, 100 percent of your focus needs to be on the meeting. When a school leader calls a meeting and facilitates it while clearly distracted, it sends an incredibly negative message to the participants—one that says this meeting isn't important and that invites them to focus on other things rather than your message.

Unclear Purpose

A meeting is ineffective when it has no clear purpose. I outlined seven different purposes at the beginning of this chapter. When you decide to have a meeting, know why it needs to be called. What purpose will the meeting serve? More importantly, what is it that you want accomplished by the end of the meeting? Every meeting must have a purpose—otherwise, what is the point of the meeting? Think about what is it about your message that necessitates a face-to-face meeting; that is, can you communicate just as effectively via an email or a phone call? When you decide to bring a group of people into a room for a meeting, know and understand why. Which of the seven purposes are you trying to achieve?

Too Much Talking

School leaders make meetings ineffective really quickly when they talk too much. Remember, meetings are not presentations. Meetings are a forum for two-way communication, which means you should limit your talking time so you can let others speak. When preparing for meetings, keep this in mind. Be purposeful about what exactly you're going to say so you don't overtalk. Prepare those critical questions that you know will start the discussion so you can get the feedback that you need in that meeting.

No Closure

The ending of every meeting is probably the most important part. This is truly when you will know if you met the purpose of the meeting or not. In ineffective meetings, closure is lacking. In other words, after a lot of two-way communication during the meeting, the meeting just kind of ends with no clear direction on what the next steps are or what any of the discussion means moving forward. As a result, nothing changes after the meeting, which makes it a waste of time—because again, what was the point of the meeting if nothing changes or nothing happens at the end of it?

Time Issues

Meetings can become ineffective when they do not start or end on time. If you schedule a meeting before school at 7:45 a.m., then begin at 7:45 a.m. If you say you will start a meeting after school at 3:30 p.m., then begin at 3:30 p.m. When you don't honor or respect the time you set for meetings, you give permission to people to come late. And likewise, if you've scheduled forty-five minutes, then make it a forty-five-minute meeting. Not honoring these times gives people the message that you do not value their time or that you did not plan well.

Meeting for the Sake of Meeting

Schools typically have set, recurring meetings throughout the year, such as department meetings, leadership meetings, and PTA meetings. These meetings could be the first Tuesday of every month or every first and third Thursday of every month. These meetings can become ineffective when school leaders meet just for the sake of meeting because the dates have been on the calendar. Just because the meeting dates have been predetermined is not enough of a reason to meet, nor is it a valid purpose for a meeting.

Audience Behavior and Meeting Success

The characteristics that I have listed are ones that you have control over. They are all things you can do (or not do) during and before meetings that can cause them to be ineffective. But you're not the only one in the meeting; the behavior of other participants in the meeting can make them ineffective; you must also be aware of this in order to address it. Other adults (and, of course, students) can behave in ways that deter you from achieving your purpose. You can use the reproducible "Addressing Behaviors in Meetings" (page 56) before every meeting to reflect on whether these behaviors could show up in your meeting and what you can do about it. Being prepared to address the following behaviors will help to minimize them.

The Talkers

There will always be some people in your meeting who just can't stop talking. These people can ramble on and on about a topic, or they may say the same thing in multiple ways and multiple times. This behavior prevents others from talking because the talkers take up all the time. This is ineffective obviously because you don't hear from everyone at the meeting, so the information you do receive is from limited perspectives.

The Soundless

On the other hand, you may have people who don't ever speak up. They come to every meeting you invite them to, but they never say anything. Their voices are never heard, and you never benefit from their input or ideas. This can make the meeting ineffective because you are missing out on the feedback of an entire group of people. Two-way communication in meetings means you need to hear from everyone.

The Resistors

There could be people in the meeting who resist everything that you bring up. They poke holes in every idea and find ways to avoid doing anything different. Now, you do assuredly need to hear all the downsides of any initiative or any idea, but resistors take it a step further by making it their mission to block *anything* new from happening. They want to maintain the status quo and will do anything to stop any kind of change from happening.

The Advocates

Sometimes when people attend meetings, they are there to advocate for someone or a group of people. For example, a parent may be in the meeting with you to advocate for his or her child. A teacher may in the meeting with you to advocate for his or her department. Although their purpose is to advocate, remember the purpose of your meeting. Too much advocating can sometimes lead to ineffective meetings because the advocate's perspective can prevent people from listening to the multiple views or discussion items that are on the table. As a result, it can make it difficult to come to any kind of a compromise when it's decision-making time.

The Rebels

There are always people who either walk in late to meetings or leave early. Sure, sometimes an emergency occurs, but when there is always somebody coming in late or leaving early, that's an issue. The perception it gives is that this meeting isn't that important. And if some people can come late or leave early, then maybe others can too. Or it tells the rule followers that their time is not that valuable. These other people make the effort to come on time and leave when the meeting concludes—but what if others don't have the same expectations?

The Doubters

When people in your meeting don't trust you or the others, the meeting has potential for being ineffective. These people will not talk freely for fear of being judged or may be argumentative with whatever it is they feel strongly about. Lack of trust among members will make a meeting go south very quickly.

The Distracted

Think about the last meeting you led. How many people were on their phones? How many people brought their laptops and were either checking email or perhaps just surfing the internet? How many people were grading papers? Granted, you have lots to do too, but during a meeting that you are leading, distracted behavior will increase the chances of that meeting becoming ineffective. How can it be effective when people in your meeting clearly are not paying attention? Or they are behaving in ways that tell you they would rather be somewhere else?

The Side Talkers

These people always partake in a sidebar conversation during meetings. Side talkers will not speak up for the entire audience to hear what they have to say; they just say it quietly to whoever is sitting next to them. Whether they are making jokes or whispering comments about something, they can very quickly derail meetings because they draw the attention and focus of those who are nearby with what they are saying or what they are laughing about.

The Interrupters

When people interrupt, this can lead to the meeting becoming ineffective. Those who were sharing ideas or brainstorming do not get an opportunity to finish their thoughts, which can make them feel upset because they did not get to say what they wanted to say.

The Pessimists

There are people who, no matter what, see the glass as half empty. These people view everything in a negative light. This behavior can completely kill the tone of a meeting because the negativity can spread. Their comments and general opinions on issues are unenthusiastic. This can make meetings ineffective because this behavior may prevent others from accomplishing tasks or being excited about an idea.

Problematic Behaviors

Now that we have reviewed these behaviors (some of which surely you have seen!), it is, as I mentioned earlier, your job to address them so you can ensure the meetings you lead and facilitate are effective. As a school leader, you must have the leadership skills to navigate these behaviors—otherwise it doesn't matter how well you plan for meetings; there is a chance those meetings will not accomplish what you want them to accomplish because of these behaviors. So, what are those leadership skills? Refer to the reproducible "Addressing Behaviors in Meetings" (page 56) as you read the following strategies and reflect on which are likely to work for your audience.

Communicate Expectations

First and foremost, you should clearly communicate what your expectations are for meetings. Clearly state the importance of starting and ending on time. Clearly state the rules or norms for your meetings. Clearly state what behaviors are not okay during your meetings. It's easy and natural to assume that your audience members know how to behave in meetings, but that may not be the case. You must explicitly state which behaviors are not acceptable.

Hold Attendees Accountable

Second, you must have the courage to address behaviors that do not align with your expectations—which you have already communicated prior to the meeting. In other words, once you have communicated your expectations for your meetings, then hold people accountable when they do not meet those expectations. This is critical. If you do not hold people accountable for their behaviors during meetings, then you are giving them permission to behave or communicate in any way they please. Consultant John C. Fetzer (2009) states, "The facilitator must be part diplomat and part headmaster. She or he is empowered to stop any discussions that meander, to remind people of the ground rules, and to keep the meeting moving forward" (p. 1827). That is part of your job as the school leader.

Elements of Effective Meetings

There are many things you have direct control over to help make your meetings effective. These are all things you can do to better prepare for a great meeting. Remember, you are calling these meetings and people are coming to you for a purpose. Put the time into preparing for every meeting so that it is efficient, and you walk out of it knowing it went well.

Beginning—What to Do Before the Meeting

There is much you can do before the meeting even starts to ensure its success. These may seem like basic reminders, but taking some extra time to check that you've accounted for all of them can make a huge difference.

Purpose

As I discussed earlier in this chapter, every meeting must serve a purpose. Examine the different purposes that I outline on page 37—one of those should be the reason for your meeting. When you are crystal clear on what the purpose is, chances are you will be that much more able to ensure you achieve it.

Audience

Once you know the purpose of your meeting, think through whom you will invite. The people you are inviting will help you achieve the purpose of your meeting. Do you need a cross section of people, or do you need a group of people from the same department? If you need input from a big group of people, then give a survey to everyone—but I recommend that the actual meeting should be with a group of two to about twelve people. Because remember, in the meeting, you will engage your group in two-way dialogue, and that becomes difficult if too many people are involved (another reason why faculty meetings or staff meetings should be treated like presentations instead of meetings). Any time I have been in a meeting with more than twelve people, everyone tries to speak while nobody listens, or just a handful of people speak while the others are not providing any input. Author Paul Axtell (2018) actually goes even further to suggest meetings should not have more than eight people. He argues when you have too many people in a meeting, the following issues occur:

- There is not enough time for everyone to participate in the conversation.

- Rich back and forth debate is replaced by shallow comments.

- Information-sharing and catch-ups distract from addressing higher priority issues.

- People become more guarded and less candid.

- Tough topics and decisions are not put on the agenda, then are dealt with off-line instead.

As a result, people often lose respect for the meeting which leads to less preparation, participation, and action. It can become a vicious downward cycle. (Axtell, 2018)

In fact, Bailey (2013) states that the more people you have in meetings, the higher the chances are of productivity going down.

Therefore, in order to ensure you don't have a lot of people in your meeting, go back to the purpose of your meeting and whom specifically you will need in that meeting to help fulfill that purpose.

Agenda

Every meeting must always have an agenda. Yes—every meeting! According to Nicholas C. Romano and Jay F. Nunamaker Jr. (2001), "Agendas are considered to be essential framing devices for meetings and the lack of one suggests inadequate planning" (p. 10). Sometimes, you can provide that agenda to the group so all are aware, and sometimes that agenda may be just for you. For example, when meeting with a parent to resolve an issue, you do not need to give him or her a copy of your agenda, but you should still have it so you know how to lead that meeting. In that case, your agenda may include the following four items.

1. Thank parent for coming in.

2. Invite parent to share his or her concerns.

3. Brainstorm solutions together.

4. Review plan of action moving forward.

It may seem trivial to put an agenda together just for you, but this will help keep the meeting on track, thereby helping it be more effective.

In addition, it is helpful to get the agenda out to the participants ahead of time. This gives them a chance to be better prepared for the meeting, increasing the chances of that meeting being productive and efficient: "The best predictor of the success of a meeting may be a written agenda distributed in advance" (Romano & Nunamaker, 2001, p. 10). The reproducible "Agenda Template" (page 53) is an example of a template that you could use or modify for your meetings.

Needs

For every meeting, think about what you need ahead of time. For example, will you provide refreshments or food? Will there be handouts? Chart paper and markers maybe? Or will you bring data from a survey or from something else? Will you need certain documentation or policies if you are meeting to resolve a conflict? Having all your needs for the meeting prepared ahead of time helps make the meeting effective. Also think about what is necessary for the people you are meeting with. Do they need to read something before coming? Do they need to have reviewed something before the meeting? If so, be sure to remind them a day before the meeting so they are more likely to come to the meeting prepared. An example of that reminder follows.

> As a reminder, we are meeting tomorrow to brainstorm how we want to change our school website. Please review the sample websites attached to this email to get some ideas. In addition, please review the survey results from our stakeholders to see their input for our website.

These kinds of reminders are important because it is hard to make the meeting effective if you or the people in your meeting come unprepared. In order to think about your needs for the meeting, go back to your purpose. What kinds of items or materials will you need to meet your purpose?

Where and When

In schools, sometimes the places where you can hold meetings are limited, but whichever room you have them in, ensure it has the appropriate materials that you need and comfortable seating for whatever seating arrangement you choose. Arrange seats in a manner that will promote collaboration and allow the audience to see the board or other locations where you display pertinent information (MacLeod, 2011). In addition, think about when to schedule the meeting. Les MacLeod (2011) advises to always avoid those dreaded Monday morning or Friday afternoon meetings. Whenever you decide to hold the meeting, provide as much advance notice as possible to help make the meeting effective. Based on the results of their research, Boris Eisenbart, Massimo Garbuio, Daniele Mascia, and Federica Morandi (2016) offer the following suggestion: "Because of the reflection process that takes place before a meeting, meeting scheduling affects both decision speed and decision-making effectiveness" (p. 32). In other words, you are likely to reach better decisions if your audience has had time to process the agenda and the purpose of the meeting before coming to the meeting.

Middle—What to Do During the Meeting

Now that you've sufficiently prepared for the meeting, it's time to focus on the meeting itself. Even with preparation, your actions during the meeting are important to its success.

Rules

Every meeting needs to have rules to govern this collaborative work time. Sometimes the rules are the same for every meeting, and other times you may have different rules depending on who is present and what the purpose is. But every meeting needs to begin with a statement of the rules. For example, you can begin the meeting with the following.

> Before we begin our meeting, I wanted to go over some ground rules. Please be present; in other words, put your phones and laptops away. In addition, please don't engage in sidebar conversation. Refrain from talking longer than three minutes at a time so we don't have people who dominate the meeting. And lastly, keep an open and positive mind during our discussion.

Other examples of rules could be those that pertain to how to handle decision making—do you go by consensus or majority rules? Another rule could be about how to ensure everyone's voices are heard. You can call these rules, norms, or protocols.

As mentioned earlier, the most important thing you can do after you clearly state your rules is to address the rule breakers. When someone does not follow a rule that you articulated, what will you do? Knowing what to do in this situation is critical to ensure your meeting is productive and successful. Think about how teachers address students when they do not behave appropriately. What are those strategies? This can include a friendly reminder, redirection, or even just reminding them of the rules. Employ those classroom management strategies in your meetings. But if the behavior continues, have a one-to-one conversation with the person or persons after the meeting.

Share the Purpose

When you state the rules, also share the purpose of the meeting. It helps all members of the group to know what exactly they are trying to accomplish. When they are aware of why they are there, it is more likely they will fulfill that desired outcome. You also verify the importance of the meeting by showing that it has a clear purpose. All members of the group should be aware of what they need to accomplish by the end.

Helpers

Helpers can be useful to you during the meeting. You can assign people to help you, or you can ask for volunteers—or bring an assistant (maybe your secretary) to help you with the tasks you do not need to focus on, like distributing handouts when necessary or getting the materials ready. This could also include taking notes—either privately or publicly so everyone can see what is being recorded. During the meeting, your job is to stay focused on the task and on facilitating. You can rely on someone else to do the rest.

Focus

Because a meeting is communication between or among two or more people, during that time, you must ensure that you keep that communication focused and on task. The communication in the meetings should always focus more on solutions than on complaints. MacLeod (2011) shares the 80:20 rule, by which 80 percent of the time during meetings should be spent on solving an issue and 20 percent or less should be spent on discussing the issue itself. Focus also means being attentive to the time the group is spending on discussion before making a decision. School leaders can't allow discussions to go on and on—at some point you need to call for a decision. Henning Bang, Synne L. Fuglesang, Mariann R. Ovesen, and Dag Erik

Eilertsen (2010) use the term *focused communication*, which they define as "the degree to which group members stick to the issue during a management meeting; that is, whether a group refrains from digression and/or goal irrelevant behaviors" (p. 254). In their study, they find that there is a positive relationship between focused communication and team effectiveness in meetings. If school leaders can keep the focus on the agenda and on fulfilling the purpose of the meeting, that increases the chances of the group having an effective meeting.

Participation

Everyone in the meeting should participate—this is what makes meetings different than presentations. Plan specifically how this will happen. What engaging and interactive strategies can you use to ensure everyone in the meeting is participating and adding value, which in turn helps make the meeting effective? Ava S. Butler (2014) provides several suggestions on how to involve participants in meetings. The reproducible "Interactive Strategies for Meetings" (page 57) outlines some of those techniques to help facilitate engaging and interactive meetings.

End—What to Do at the End of the Meeting

And now it's time to stick the landing. Ending your meeting the right way is essential. Just like there are strategies for the beginning and middle of meetings, there are some strategies that you can use to end your meetings.

Purpose Check

At the end of the meeting, check to see if you have met your purpose. Summarize what the group discussed in the meeting and then review your purpose to verify that you have fulfilled it. Instilling everyone with this sense of accomplishment and satisfaction is a great way to conclude the meeting. Always remember that a successful meeting is when you have fulfilled your purpose for the meeting.

Homework Assignments

At the end of the meeting, you may sometimes need to assign homework, or specific tasks that people need to be responsible for. This could be anything, but the point here is that whatever the group discussed or decided on, someone needs to follow through with it or do something about it. Publicly assign homework so there is accountability after the meeting is over.

Notes

It is beneficial to email summary notes, or meeting minutes, from your meeting to everyone about twenty-four to forty-eight hours after concluding (or if the notetaker uses an online platform, he or she can share them right away during the meeting). These notes should capture the key decisions the group makes during the meeting, along with the follow-up regarding who is responsible for what. If the group does not come to any decisions, then the notes should capture the key discussion items that you communicate and, again, the follow-up to that discussion—what comes next? The agenda template shown in the reproducible "Agenda Template" (page 53) has a built-in notes section, along with a follow-up section at the end.

Summary

Meetings are a critical part of your job—if you used figure 2.1 (page 36) to tally up the number of hours you personally spend in meetings, you have seen the amount of time that you devote to this task. As a result, it's essential that your meetings are effective, efficient, and productive so they are not a waste of anyone's time. Meetings are when you gather people around you to communicate and discuss vital issues or concerns—so make them productive. Experts sum it up like this: "Meetings are essential for enabling collaboration, creativity, and innovation. They often foster relationships and ensure proper information exchange" (Perlow et al., 2017). When people come together in a meeting that is productive, they are likely to leave with a sense of accomplishment, which fosters success for your school. This chapter reviews strategies to help maximize your meetings so that every meeting you facilitate is a successful one. The reproducible "Meeting Planning Document" (page 54) is a checklist you can use when preparing for your meetings to ensure you have incorporated these strategies.

Reflection Questions

1. What ineffective behavior do you display in meetings? How can you minimize it?

2. Before calling a meeting, what questions should you ask yourself? What steps will you take to begin preparing for the meeting?

3. What behavior do you see most often that contributes to an ineffective meeting? How will you now address it?

4. What is one strategy you can use to ensure everyone in your meeting is actively engaged?

The School Leader's Communication Challenge: Meetings

The following challenge is designed to be flexible. Depending on your needs and upcoming schedule, you can pick one meeting that you have scheduled this month and follow each step closely, or you can use the provided resources to help you reflect on all of your meetings this month.

Challenge	Notes
• Create an agenda (use the reproducible "Agenda Template," page 53). • Start filling out the reproducible "Meeting Planning Document" (page 54) before the meeting and keep adding to it during and afterward. • Before the meeting, review the reproducible "Addressing Behaviors in Meetings" (page 56) to plan how to react to problematic conduct by attendees. • After the meeting, use the reproducible "Interactive Strategies for Meetings" (page 57) to see if you did what you said you would do. • Conduct the SWOT analysis (page 58) and monitor your goal.	

Agenda Template

School Mission

Date: _____ Time: _____

Rules for Our Meeting

1. Begin and end on time.
2. Come prepared.
3. Stay focused on the meeting.
4. Follow through with tasks assigned.

Purpose for This Meeting: _____

Agenda

Agenda Items	Notes

Assigned Tasks	Person Responsible	Deadline

Did we accomplish our purpose? _____

Connecting Through Leadership © 2020 Solution Tree Press • SolutionTree.com
Visit **go.SolutionTree.com/leadership** to download this free reproducible.

Meeting Planning Document

Preparing for the Beginning

What is my purpose for the meeting?
What do I want to have accomplished by the end of the meeting?
Whom will I invite to the meeting?
How will those people help achieve the purpose of the meeting?
Have I created and shared an agenda for the meeting? ☐ Yes ☐ No
What materials do I need for the meeting?
Have I sent out reminders about the meeting? ☐ Yes ☐ No
Have I told people what they need to bring or do prior to the meeting? ☐ Yes ☐ No

Connecting Through Leadership © 2020 Solution Tree Press • SolutionTree.com
Visit **go.SolutionTree.com/leadership** to download this free reproducible.

Preparing for the Middle

What are the rules for the meeting?
Have I shared the purpose of the meeting with everyone? ☐ Yes ☐ No
What can I ask for help with or assign participants to do during the meeting?
What behaviors might I address that could prevent us from achieving our purpose?
What interactive strategy might I include in the meeting to ensure everyone participates and is engaged?

Preparing for the End

Did we meet our purpose for holding the meeting? ☐ Yes ☐ No
What homework did I assign to people in order to ensure that they follow through?
Have I emailed or posted the notes to everyone within forty-eight hours after the meeting? ☐ Yes ☐ No

Connecting Through Leadership © 2020 Solution Tree Press • SolutionTree.com
Visit **go.SolutionTree.com/leadership** to download this free reproducible.

REPRODUCIBLE

Addressing Behaviors in Meetings

Behaviors by Audience	I May See These Behaviors	How Will I Respond?
The Talkers		
The Soundless		
The Resistors		
The Advocates		
The Rebels		
The Doubters		
The Distracted		
The Side Talkers		
The Interrupters		
The Pessimists		

Interactive Strategies for Meetings

Strategy	Description
Card Clusters	Participants write their thoughts (about a question or prompt) individually on sticky notes. Put all the sticky notes up on a wall, and then the group clusters them by similar ideas and themes.
Milestones	First, create a time line on the board. Participants think about a big event that occurred (a life event, something that happened at school, or something that happened in their team) and then write it on a sticky note. Participants then put their sticky notes on the time line, and everyone shares by going from the beginning to the current time to share the major events that have taken place.
Passing Notes	Present an incomplete sentence prompt, a question, or a quote. Participants each add their thoughts to a sheet of paper and then pass it on to the next person. Once everyone has read everyone's thoughts, hold an open discussion about the themes that emerge.
Role Play or Skits	Insert skits or role play into meetings to allow participants to experience certain concepts and understand different perspectives.
Edward de Bono's (1985) Six Thinking Hats	Participants wear different hats to provide feedback based on particular perspectives. The hats are logic (facts); optimism (benefits); devil's advocate (difficulties); emotion (feelings); creativity (new ideas); and management (ensure participants are fulfilling the roles of their hats). If you want to get creative, you could bring a variety of hats—or you could just have the audience use a sticker to name their hat and put it on their shirts (like name badges).
The Five Whys	Pose a problem and ask participants why. After they answer, ask why again. Continue to ask why three more times to uncover the various layers before getting into solutions.
Ball Throwing	Use a tennis ball or a stuffed animal to throw to participants throughout the meeting. Whoever you throw to is the person who speaks.
Study Tables	Have a printout of a few different articles at different tables. Participants go to a table, read the article, and then take turns sharing their learning with the whole group.
Ignite	Participants prepare two-minute presentations with personal pictures of themselves that tell their stories. You can have one or two participants give their presentations at each meeting until everyone has had a turn. Through this activity, participants learn more about one another.
Keep and Throw	Pose a question and ask some participants what ideas they want to keep and ask another group what ideas they want to throw away. Switch sides and ask again.

Source: Butler, A. S. (2014). Mission critical meetings: 81 practical facilitation techniques. *Tucson, AZ: Wheatmark.*

Reference

de Bono, E. (1985). *Six thinking hats.* New York: Little, Brown.

Connecting Through Leadership © 2020 Solution Tree Press • SolutionTree.com
Visit **go.SolutionTree.com/leadership** to download this free reproducible.

SWOT Analysis on My Meeting Facilitation Skills

Strengths	Weaknesses	Opportunities	Threats
What are you good at when it comes to facilitating meetings?	When facilitating a meeting, what would you consider your weaknesses?	How can you get better at facilitating meetings so that every meeting is productive? So that everyone walks out feeling a sense of accomplishment?	Think of how unforseen circumstances can affect your meetings—how can you prepare?

My goal for future meetings:

Connecting Through Leadership © 2020 Solution Tree Press • SolutionTree.com
Visit **go.SolutionTree.com/leadership** to download this free reproducible.

CHAPTER 3
Communicating Through Tough Conversations

Be brave enough to start a conversation that matters.

—Margaret Wheatley

A big part of your job as a school leader is to be able to communicate effectively during tough conversations. Tough conversations are those where you know the other person is not going to be pleased with your message, the message you need to communicate is uncomfortable or awkward, and you know you may hurt the other person's feelings with your message. In short, these conversations are "a discussion between two or more people where (1) stakes are high, (2) opinions vary, and (3) emotions run strong" (Patterson, Grenny, McMillan, & Switzler, 2002, p. 3). Tough conversations can lead to angry responses, tears, or silence. Tough conversations are those where you know if it doesn't go well, the consequences for your school could be negative.

This chapter begins by discussing the purpose of tough conversations and then describes when those conversations are necessary. I outline barriers to having tough conversations and then provide a structure for effective tough conversations. After that, I share elements of ineffective tough conversations and then provide several tips to help school leaders have effective tough conversations. As always, I conclude the chapter with questions for reflection.

59

Purpose of Tough Conversations

If tough conversations are so tough, why do we have to have them? Although it may be easier to avoid engaging in tough conversations, not having them could be detrimental to your school and, therefore, your students. Shouldering the responsibility of these conversations is an essential part of being a good school leader, and part of what differentiates leaders from managers. Nobody said it would be easy!

Timothy D. Kanold (2011) describes the difference between management and leadership: "Management requires the courage to monitor . . . Leadership requires you to respond to what you learn during the monitoring process" (p. 39). Remember why you are a school leader—to ensure all your students succeed by learning at high levels. As a school leader, you are there not to keep the adults in your school content but rather to see that all the adults in your school are working toward ensuring all students are learning. And when someone is not doing that, you must intervene by holding tough conversations. Ultimately, the goal for any tough conversation is to change the behavior that is causing the conversation to occur in the first place so that all of you can continue to do your work to enhance student learning.

As stated, the main reason school leaders need to have tough conversations is because someone is doing something that hinders student learning. When you allow destructive behaviors to continue, you are jeopardizing your own purpose as a school leader. Richard DuFour, Rebecca DuFour, Robert Eaker, Thomas W. Many, and Mike Mattos (2016) assert, "Nothing will destroy the credibility of a leader faster than an unwillingness to address an obvious violation of what the organization contends is vital" (p. 213). Avoiding tough conversations because they are difficult is a sign of weak leadership, which ultimately will not bring about success in your school. Baruti K. Kafele (2015) states:

> You must hold your entire school community accountable for
> the pursuit of excellence, and your standards must remain
> high for each and every one involved—but especially for
> teachers. Though you must always treat teachers fairly when
> holding them accountable, your leadership must also be firmly
> established. (p. 45)

You owe it to your students to have the courage and the necessary skills to have effective conversations, no matter how tough they are. You must be the leader your students need you to be.

When to Have Tough Conversations

Sometimes you may not be clear on what warrants a tough conversation. Now that you know why tough conversations should not be avoided, let's discuss the situations or circumstances in which we need to have them.

Violation of Laws and Ethics

Many laws and systems of ethics govern the world of education. School leaders should expect that everyone complies with these laws and ethical principles. Unfortunately, there are times when staff members in a school violate those expectations. When that happens, a tough conversation must occur (and perhaps, in addition to that conversation, you will need to take other steps as required by your school district). Following are some examples of law and ethics violations that all school leaders must be prepared to address.

- Special education law
  - › Teacher does not follow the student's individualized education program (IEP).
  - › Teacher posts a list in his or her class with all the special education students' names and identifies them as receiving special education services.
  - › Teacher falsifies the data on a student's IEP.
- Family Education Rights and Privacy Act (FERPA) laws
  - › Teacher emails parents the quiz scores of all his or her students.
  - › Teacher has a student help him or her grade all the students' assignments.
  - › Teacher tells parents during open house that there is a student in the classroom who is a behavior nightmare and then proceeds to share who that student is.
- Ethics violations
  - › Teacher shares his or her political beliefs with students and tries to persuade them to be in favor of those beliefs.
  - › Teacher provides students with answers while they are taking a test.
  - › Teacher sells candy and school supplies to students for personal financial gain.

Violation of School Board Policies

Many school board policies are based on various laws and ethics while some policies are specific to a school system. Just like laws and ethics, you should expect everyone in your school to follow these rules, and if there is a violation of a board policy, then it is your responsibility to address it through a tough conversation (again, perhaps followed up by other steps as required by your school district). Following are some examples of board policy violations that you may need to address. It is important to note that sometimes these issues may overlap—a board policy violation could also be an ethical violation, or vice versa.

- Teacher does not provide schoolwork to a student who was absent due to medical reasons and gives the student a zero on that work.
- Teacher collects money from students for a field trip and keeps that money in his or her desk for several weeks.
- Teacher does not take student attendance.
- Student complains of a headache, so teacher gives the student pain-relief medicine.
- Teacher takes a sick day but then posts pictures on social media saying he or she is having a great time on a minivacation at the beach.

Violation of Local School Procedures

You are also responsible for setting up certain local school procedures to ensure your school is operating effectively and efficiently. These may be based on school district policies as well as school laws and ethics, and some procedures may just be specific to the school. Either way, this is a set of rules, just like laws, board policies, and ethics, that staff members must adhere to.

Local school procedures also include the expectations that you as a school leader have set for your staff. When someone violates these expectations, it is your responsibility to have a tough conversation in order to change the behavior so that it aligns to your expectations. Following are some examples of local school procedure violations that should result in tough conversations (and maybe other consequences as well).

- Teacher leaves students unsupervised in the classroom while he or she makes a personal phone call.
- Teacher yells, calling a student lazy and useless.
- Teacher wears inappropriate clothing to school.
- Teacher does not follow through with administering a common assessment to students after his or her collaborative team agreed on it.
- Teacher has not updated his or her classroom blog for three months.
- Teacher misses deadlines for turning things in to administration (for example, grades, forms, and so on).
- Teacher has excessive tardies or absences from work.

Negativity

In addition to violation of explicit laws, policies, ethics, or procedures, there are times when staff members can behave in ways that create a negative atmosphere in your school. You have probably encountered people in your professional life who, no matter what, are just never happy. Negativity can quickly spread to other teachers (especially the new teachers in your school), so it becomes your responsibility as the school leader to address it. Following are some examples of when you may need to have a tough conversation.

- Teacher makes negative posts about your school on social media for other teachers, central office personnel, board members, and parents to see.

- Teacher speaks negatively about your school to parents and students.

- Teacher makes negative comments about your school to colleagues.

Repeat Offenders

Finally, there are times when you have tough conversations with staff and the behavior does stop—for a short period of time. And then it starts back up again. With repeat offenders, those tough conversations must continue (along with other progressive discipline steps, which I will discuss later in this chapter). Just because a tough conversation took place does not mean that you never have to have it again in the future. Unfortunately, there are times when those unwanted behaviors continue despite the tough conversation. For example, a teacher continues to come to work late, or a teacher continues to miss deadlines, or a teacher still hasn't updated his or her classroom blog.

You cannot ignore repeat offenders if they continue to dismiss the school's procedures, policies, laws, or ethics. Consequently, school leaders must continue to address these behaviors, and addressing them always begins by having tough conversations.

Other Situations

In addition to tough conversations made necessary by violation of laws or ethics, school board policies, local school procedures, negativity, or repeat offenders, there are so many more situations where a tough conversation may need to occur that don't easily fall into a category. Going back to the definition at the beginning of this chapter—this conversation can occur any time when the stakes are high, opinions vary, or emotions run strong (Patterson et al., 2002). Think of any situation where any of these factors exist, and you've got yourself a tough conversation. When you need to communicate with a teacher who vehemently disagrees with you on something, when you need to communicate with a parent receiving some really bad news such as a child being retained or expelled, or when you need to communicate with someone to explain that the school will not be hiring him or her—all of these and countless others are situations that require tough conversations. School leaders face so many of these kinds of situations so frequently, but they can learn the skills to effectively handle them.

Barriers to Tough Conversations

It's entirely likely that there is a tough conversation right now that you know you need to have—but that you've been avoiding. Is there someone at your school whom you really want to say something to but haven't had a chance to do so? You know the importance of having tough conversations—these conversations are critical to getting the results you want for your students. You know when to have tough conversations—you have likely experienced more than one of the violations or failures of follow-through listed in the previous section. But why is it still so difficult to engage in tough conversations? Many school leaders know what they want to say—why not just say it? Why do school leaders sometimes prefer to avoid having the tough conversation, even though they know they shouldn't? I will discuss these barriers in detail in the following sections and provide some suggestions to help minimize those barriers. Later in this chapter, I will provide more detailed tips and strategies for having tough conversations, which may help in reducing all the barriers in the following sections.

Personal Relationships

From the moment you decided you wanted to get into school leadership, you likely heard, over and over again, about the importance of relationships, that successful leaders build positive relationships with their staff. Unfortunately, those positive relationships you work so hard to build may end up becoming the biggest barriers to having tough conversations. It's natural to worry that you might jeopardize your relationships with your staff by having tough conversations with them. What if they don't like you anymore? What if they stop talking to you?

The answer is not to avoid relationships. As you work to build relationships with your staff, remember why these connections are important. Connections matter because with them it will actually be *easier* to have those tough conversations if and when that time comes. Think back to when you were a teacher—why did you build relationships with your students? You wanted students to want to work for you. If they ever misbehaved, they would respond to your redirection *because* of your good relationship with them. Apply that same logic to your staff. You build relationships with your staff so that when you do have a tough conversation with them, they will respond appropriately to it. If you have truly earned their trust and respect, they will take your feedback in that tough conversation well *because* of your relationship.

Strategies for minimizing the effect of personal relationships on conducting tough conversations include the following.

- Be honest.
- Understand that this is not personal—you have a job to do, which is to ensure every student succeeds.

- Put your feelings aside and focus on the issue.
- Always remember why you're here—to do what is best for your students. If an adult is in the way of that, you need to have a tough conversation.
- Use the power of numbers. Maybe have someone else sit in on the conversation with you.

Fear of Confrontation

Sometimes a school leader's biggest barrier is fear of confrontation. If you generalize the personalities of educators, you can argue that educators are caregivers and want to help and serve others. Being confrontational isn't typically one of an educator's strong attributes. Chances are that when you got into teaching, you weren't thinking about school leadership—you wanted to teach and make a difference in the lives of your students. The transition into school leadership makes many school leaders realize quickly that working with adults is very different from working with students. And confronting adults about their decisions or behaviors is very different from confronting students.

Strategies for mitigating the fear of confrontation during tough conversations include the following.

- Plan and prepare ahead of time for the conversation; know what your first sentence is going to be.
- Be direct; stick to the facts.
- Anticipate possible reactions and prepare for them.

Nothing-Will-Change Attitude

School leaders sometimes avoid having tough conversations because they assume or believe the person will not change. Think about a person in your school who has displayed annoying or unproductive behaviors or attitude ever since you've known him or her. The reason this happens is because nobody before you has had the courage to have a tough conversation with that person, or there was never any follow-through after the tough conversation took place. The leaders before you may have assumed that person cannot change, and as a result, they never bothered to have the conversation. The problem is whether or not people can change; you as a school leader owe it to the students in your school to have those tough conversations. As a leader, you cannot allow people to stagnate. It is up to you to work with these educators to change behaviors for the sake of your students and your school.

Some strategies to resist this pervasive attitude include the following.

- First, make the person you need to talk to aware of the situation.
- Document every conversation to illustrate patterns.

- Set expectations and then hold him or her accountable.
- Be consistent.
- Help identify the source of the problem.

Uncomfortable Topics

You have quite likely had situations in which you avoided having a tough conversation because the topic itself was awkward and uncomfortable for you to bring up. One example of this might be having a tough conversation with a teacher because of the way he or she dresses. It could be that the clothing is very revealing or not professional enough. Or think about a situation in which you need to talk to someone who just does not understand boundaries or personal space and speaks to people while standing really close to them. Another possibility is the need to discuss with a teacher how he or she takes over meetings by being a talker and does not allow others to voice their thoughts. Uncomfortable concerns are usually difficult to bring up because it can involve embarrassing the teacher whom we are speaking with. To avoid embarrassment, it's easier to just not have that tough conversation.

Strategies for minimizing the effect of uncomfortable concerns on having tough conversations include the following.

- Be direct but sympathetic, knowing the person may feel embarrassed.
- Focus on the issue.
- Know your first sentence; go in prepared to begin the conversation.

Negative Reactions

You may have people in your school who you are not sure will react well to a tough conversation. Will they respond with anger? Will they respond by retaliating against you in some way? Will they go to your local school board or some other organization to file a formal complaint? That apprehension about how people may react or respond to the tough conversation can be a reason to avoid having it altogether. Remember that leadership is not easy. Leadership involves being courageous, and sometimes that courage means that regardless of how a teacher or staff member might react to a tough conversation, you still must have it.

Strategies for minimizing the effect of negative reactions on tough conversations include the following.

- Have this conversation with a witness present.
- Use a team approach if possible.
- Stay calm.

- Prepare for reinforcement if necessary (have certain people such as a school resource officer or another administrator on standby in case you need them).

- Arrange your room so you have a plan for escape if necessary.

- Disarm the person's emotion as much as possible by staying neutral and keeping the conversation focused on the issue.

Time Constraints

Let's face it—having tough conversations can be incredibly time consuming. Think about how much time you spend before the conversation even takes place. The time it takes debating in your head whether the issue or concern is worth bringing up or not. The time you spend thinking about how to frame it, so it goes well. The time spent analyzing the pros and cons of having the conversation. The time it takes dealing with your own anxiety or nervousness about the conversation. And of course, the time it takes to actually have the tough conversation. School leaders are busy people with busy calendars; taking time out of your schedule to have tough conversations can be another reason to avoid them because other things take precedence. The aftermath of the conversation takes up time as well, whether it includes dealing with the emotional fallout or dealing with the time it takes to document everything afterward.

Strategies for making and managing your time for tough conversations include the following.

- Get the meeting on your calendar.

- Prioritize your tasks for the day and make a to-do list that includes the conversation.

- Understand the consequences of procrastinating the conversations (the issue will get worse and could become an even bigger issue).

Elements of Ineffective Tough Conversations

Many of the barriers to having tough conversations may relate to your previous experience with them. If tough conversations you have had in the past did not result in the outcomes you wanted, it's natural to be hesitant to have more of them. But if you can diagnose the issues behind your ineffective tough conversations, you'll be much better prepared to improve your future conversations. In the following sections, I unpack each of the possible causes that can make these conversations ineffective.

Frustration

Every school leader gets frustrated sometimes. You get upset, you've just had it, or you become annoyed with certain behaviors or certain decisions your teachers make.

There's nothing wrong with feeling this way, but the worst time to have a tough conversation is when you are emotionally charged. The more frustrated you are, the less likely it is that you will lead an effective tough conversation that gets the outcome you want. This is good advice not just for professional interactions but for personal ones as well. Tough conversations are more likely to be ineffective if you have them while you are frustrated. Also, keep in mind that keeping control of your emotions is especially important when the one you're having the conversation with may not be able or willing to do so. So—wait! Wait until you have calmed down to have that tough conversation. Otherwise, you risk saying something unprofessional or that you will regret, which will make that conversation ineffective.

Lack of Preparation

As a school leader, you no doubt make multiple decisions throughout each day—some of them you make quickly while others take longer. When you spontaneously make the decision to have a tough conversation with a teacher, there is a chance it may not go well. That's because you didn't prepare. In fact, it's rare for a tough conversation to go well without preparation. Just as you have to prepare for a presentation or a meeting, you must always prepare for a tough conversation. Think about those times you rushed into a conversation and realized you did not have all the facts, or you were unaware of related situations or factors. Or have you ever begun a conversation without giving it enough thought and realized you did not know how to start or even what exactly to say? Lack of preparation will quickly lead to an ineffective tough conversation.

Procrastination

On the other hand, spending too much time preparing and waiting for the right moment can also lead to an ineffective tough conversation. Procrastinating in general is usually not good, and this type of situation is no exception. Procrastinating before a tough conversation means you're letting that behavior go (and therefore accepting it)—so that by the time you do have that conversation, it's too late. For example, if a teacher does not turn his or her grades in on time, imagine addressing it two months later. And realistically, what really happens is that when you procrastinate, too much time goes by, your schedule pulls you in too many other directions, and the tough conversation never ends up happening.

Softened Message

When you try to sugarcoat the message during the tough conversation, you may inadvertently render the conversation ineffective because you begin to give mixed messages to the teacher. Say what you need to say. You are probably familiar with the sandwich approach to delivery—say something positive, then say the tough message, and then end with something positive. The problem with this approach? Think about this message:

> I really enjoyed coming into your classroom yesterday. The use of technology made the lesson very engaging. But you need to remember that you have to be in your classroom on time so that students are not unsupervised. But when you're in the classroom, your interaction with the students is so positive. You've built a very warm and safe classroom environment.

First, the tough message you were trying to get across does not seem that serious when it's surrounded by positive comments. Second, it's easy to only hear the positive comments. When you embed your message in between positive comments, you're telling your teachers that your message isn't serious. In other words, it's not really that big of a deal. And remember the purpose of tough conversations—to elicit a change in behavior so the focus can remain on student learning. Softening the message can hinder that purpose, making the tough conversation ineffective. My recommendation is to instead just focus on the issue—when you need to have a tough conversation, think about what has happened that is making you have that tough conversation. And then have your tough conversation in which you focus only on that particular issue. Do not convolute or confuse the message by adding other unnecessary messages into it in an attempt to soften the message. Just say what needs to be said so that behavior can change.

Aggression

At the other end of the spectrum, being overly aggressive when delivering messages can be ineffective. You always want to avoid being perceived as condescending or rude. Sometimes school leaders have no problem having tough conversations because they use their authority or position of power to dominate the conversation. This is ineffective because it makes the desired outcome unlikely. When school leaders are overly aggressive, chances are that they will use the wrong words (such as profanity or offensive language), their tone will be unprofessional (possibly including yelling or sarcasm), or they will include content that did not need to be said. These tactics are more likely to increase defensiveness and shut down your teachers—neither of which is going to help them change their behaviors. Author Susan Scott (2004) suggests to "learn to deliver the message without the load" (p. 199). Here are some examples she offers to describe that load.

- Blaming
- Name-calling or labeling
- Using sarcasm

- Blowing things out of proportion
- Threatening or intimidating
- Exaggerating
- Saying "If I were you . . ."

Barbara Pachter and Denise Cowie (2017) advise leaders, "Explain the situation without using aggressive language. Be honest without being cruel" (p. 142).

Structure of Effective Tough Conversations

Just like every presentation and meeting needs to have a clear structure, so do the tough conversations you plan to have. Every tough conversation needs to have a clear beginning, a clear middle, and a clear end.

Clear Beginning

At the beginning of the conversation, explain what your expectations are. This should be a review, since you will have already shared expectations at the beginning of the school year or at some point since when introducing a new rule or policy. For example, say you are having a tough conversation with a teacher because he or she does not respond to parents in a timely fashion. The parents are upset, and they have been contacting you. When you sit down with this teacher, start by stating your expectations regarding parent-teacher communication. It might sound something like this: "As are you aware, according to our faculty handbook, under the communication section on page 13, teachers are to respond to parent inquiries within twenty-four to forty-eight business hours." The important point to remember here is that this should not be the first time this teacher is hearing about this expectation. You should always communicate all your expectations (preferably in writing in a faculty handbook). Here's another example. Think about a teacher who never posts his or her learning targets on the board. The beginning of your conversation would sound something like this: "As you are aware, according to our faculty handbook, in our instructional expectation section on page 20, teachers are required to have learning targets posted on the board for students to see."

Clear Middle

The middle of the tough conversation is the big punch. This is when you state what the problem is. This is when you explain how your teacher is not meeting the expectation that you stated in the beginning of the conversation. The middle of your tough conversation is the hardest part because this is where you are going to tell your teacher why you needed to have this conversation in the first place. So, let's go back to the first two examples. If the reason for talking with the teacher is that he or she is not responding to parents in a timely fashion, then this is what you would say: "The parent contacted you via email on February 12. Today is February 20, and you still have not responded to this parent."

For the second example in which the teacher does not have learning targets posted in the classroom, that message could sound like this: "I was in your classroom this morning, and I did not see any learning targets posted." The middle of your message needs to be crystal clear as you explain what the teacher did to violate a policy or procedure. This is where it helps to be direct. Say exactly what the issue is as clearly and directly as possible.

Remember, there is a reason you are having this conversation, and this is the time to say exactly what that is. What exactly did the person do that required this conversation? You should know this answer before you even go into this tough conversation—it should be a part of your preparation. In addition to being prepared and focused on the issue, ensure you manage your emotions during the conversation. Being direct does not mean being disrespectful or rude; you should always be professional and respectful, but keep a tight focus on your point as you communicate your message.

Clear End

The end of the tough conversation is when you reiterate the expectation and clearly state what you need the person to do moving forward. There should be no question about what it is that you need that teacher to do. So again, if we go back to the example of the teacher not responding to the parent, you would end the tough conversation by saying, "I expect you to respond to this parent ASAP, and moving forward, I want to reiterate the expectation that you are to respond to parent inquiries within twenty-four to forty-eight business hours." For the other example of not having learning targets posted in the classroom, you would end that tough conversation by saying, "I expect you to get those learning targets up in your classroom by the end of today, and moving forward, I expect to see them every day in your classroom."

Summarizing the Structure of Tough Conversations

So now, let's put beginning, middle, and end together. The first scenario, in which the teacher does not respond to the parent, would go like this:

> As are you aware, according to our faculty handbook, under
> the communication section on page 13, teachers are to respond
> to parent inquiries within twenty-four to forty-eight business
> hours. The parent contacted you via email on February 12,
> today is February 20, and you still have not responded to
> this parent. I expect you to respond to this parent ASAP, and

> moving forward, I want to reiterate the expectation that you
> are to respond to parent inquiries within twenty-four to forty-
> eight business hours.

Now, let's look at the second scenario, in which the teacher does not have learning targets posted in his or her classroom:

> As you are aware, according to our faculty handbook, in
> our instructional expectation section on page 20, teachers
> are required to have learning targets posted on the board
> for students to see. I was in your classroom this morning, and
> I did not see any learning targets posted. I expect you to get
> those learning targets up in your classroom by the end of
> today, and moving forward, I expect to see them every day in
> your classroom.

Remember, this structure for having tough conversations is for teachers and other staff members in your school building who are violating an expectation, policy, or procedure that you have clearly communicated. Those tough conversations have a clear beginning, a clear middle, and a clear end so that by the time you have said your message, teachers or staff members are crystal clear on what they did, and what they need to do moving forward.

This structure does minimize the opportunity for a two-way conversation—which will work for some situations. However, there are of course times when a two-way conversation is necessary as well in order to get the person's side of the story. In that situation, the framework to follow would look like this.

- State the expectation.
- Explain the problem—how the person did not meet the expectation.
- Allow the person to share his or her perspective.
- Close by reiterating your expectations moving forward.

Connecting Through Tough Conversations

Communication is all about connecting with people. It may seem difficult to imagine that having tough conversations in which you hold people accountable will allow you to connect with them. As mentioned previously, sometimes school leaders avoid having tough conversations because they are afraid this could jeopardize the relationships they've built. I will share that from my experience, most people appreciate directness and being held accountable. They may not tell you that, but when some time has passed, most appreciate that you helped them grow. If anything, they will appreciate your honesty and consistency.

Think about the people whom you don't have tough conversations with because they always follow your expectations. Reflect on how you connect with those people when they see that you hold the people who don't follow expectations accountable. Lastly, always remember why you are the school leader. Your purpose is to ensure every student in your building is successful, and it's up to you to create a culture that allows that to happen. Yes, dealing with adults can be much harder than dealing with students, but that's the job you signed up for when you became a school leader. If all of the adults in your building are great and always do what they need to and they have no area for growth—then why are you there?

Elements of Effective Tough Conversations

As mentioned previously, there are situations when you will need to let the person on the other side of your tough conversation share his or her perspective in order to feel heard. However, many situations are quite straightforward, and you just want to say, "Here's the expectation, here's what you did, and here's what I need you to do moving forward," and that may not always happen. Conversations are rarely one-sided—there is a strong chance that during the course of delivering this message, inevitably, the teacher or staff member is going to have something to say (however, using this structure for your tough conversation could minimize the dialogue). This section provides you with some tips and suggestions how to conduct effective tough conversations.

Be Proactive

You will never have a school year in which a teacher or staff member does not violate a rule or a policy or just make a bad decision. There's always something. A good school leader is proactive and is always prepared for these situations. In order to have successful and effective tough conversations, there is some preparation work you should do—and this preparation can also help minimize the need to have tough conversations in the first place.

Set Clear Expectations

Before you start having tough conversations with your faculty or staff members about breaking certain rules, you have an obligation to clearly state what the rules are. As I discuss in chapter 1 (page 7), you can give presentations about expectations, policies, procedures, and so on at the beginning of the year or any other time that is appropriate, such as when you introduce a new policy. You should also do this through your school's faculty handbook, which you update, share, and revisit every year, and which teachers and staff members can refer to anytime.

Have a Process

In addition to communicating your expectations, make sure you have a clear process for what happens when any of those rules or procedures are not followed. What happens if someone violates that policy? Your teachers and staff members need to know this policy up front. What happens the first time, what happens the second time, and what happens the third time? An example of the process could be:

- **First violation**—Warning
- **Second violation**—Warning with letter
- **Third violation**—Disciplinary letter

I recommend creating this process in collaboration with your staff so they feel connected to it (see the reproducible "Our Response to Handbook Violations," page 81). In this process, the tough conversation occurs at every step—but during the warning phase, it may take place in the teacher's classroom where you remind the teacher of the expectation, what he or she did, and your expectations moving forward, stressing that this is a warning. At the second step, the conversation could take place in your office, in the same format, but now you follow the conversation up with a letter.

The benefit of clearly communicating this process at the beginning of the year is that teachers and staff members see that not only are you being direct about your expectations but you're also being direct about what happens if they do not meet those expectations—and it allows for that consistency to happen. Doing the work up front minimizes the times you will need to have tough conversations because teachers understand the expectations and consequences. This kind of proactive work also helps the tough conversation go more smoothly because you are just following up on what you said you would do, so there are no surprises.

Be Consistent

It should not matter who is violating the school's expectations. The rules and consequences apply to everyone equally. When you pick and choose whom you are going to hold accountable, you are damaging your integrity and the trust that others have in you. It is easier to be consistent when all you have to do throughout the school year is follow what you said in the beginning—here are the rules, and here is what happens when they are broken. In addition, consistency will help make tough conversations into a much less daunting task. It will help minimize those barriers mentioned earlier because you will know what to do anytime someone does not follow through on something. Your tough conversations are more likely to be successful because teachers and staff members will see that you're just doing what you said you would do.

Train Others

It will help you as a school leader to have more people in your school who can have tough conversations with each other. This takes some of the burden from you and helps instill a sense of connection and community throughout the school since more people are invested in keeping things running smoothly. Take the time to provide professional development—at least to all your teacher leaders to help them hold their colleagues accountable. Many times, teacher leaders just do not know where to start or how to say what they need to say. Help them, guide them, and show them. Invest in teaching your teacher leaders how to have these tough conversations; sometimes they can resolve issues before they even come to you.

Before the Conversation

Despite all your efforts to be proactive and preventative, there will always be someone who requires a tough conversation. Phil Harkins (2017) compares the importance of preparing for these conversations to when a lawyer prepares for court or a musician rehearses before a performance: "Walking into a difficult conversation without adequate preparation can feel like approaching a hornet's nest without protection" (p. 83). The following tips will help you better prepare for that tough conversation.

Set an Agenda

Always create an agenda for yourself for that tough conversation. Know what you're going to say in the beginning, middle, and end. Have your key points down on paper so you know how to steer that conversation. See the reproducible "Agenda Template" (page 82) for a sample agenda outline you can use. Remember this is just for you to plan your conversation—it is not to share with anyone.

Use Appropriate Timing

Think about the timing of the tough conversation. Sometimes it is better to wait until Friday afternoon so the person has the weekend to recover from it, or sometimes it may be good to have it on a Monday. Don't just spontaneously have the tough conversation—think through the best time to have it.

Talk Face to Face

The tough conversation should always be face to face. It's easy to just hide behind a computer and email what you want to say, but there is value in connecting with someone in a face-to-face conversation. A tough message is one you need to communicate face to face because you also want to communicate the fact that ensuring the issue gets resolved means that much to you.

Consider Including Another Person

When you have this face-to-face conversation, will there be anybody else in the office with you? Do you want to have another school administrator present? The purpose of having someone else in the room is not so you both can bully that teacher, but rather to witness the conversation. Also, it's a great way to get feedback on how you did afterward.

Prepare a First Line

Always prepare for that first sentence. What is the first thing you will say? This first sentence will determine the direction of the conversation. For example, are you going to start with small talk or get right into it? I recommend getting right into it because that helps focus the conversation. Think about the following scenarios—what would your first sentence be?

- Teacher dresses unprofessionally.
- Custodian is leaving early without prior approval.
- Teacher yells at a parent.

During the Conversation

Once you have prepared for the conversation, it's time to do the talking. The following tips can help you during that conversation depending on how the teacher or staff member is responding.

Use Silence to Your Advantage

Silence can be awkward in any conversation, especially a tough conversation. However, you can also think of silence as a good thing when it allows your teacher or staff member to process what you just shared with him or her. Scott (2004) states, "The more emotionally loaded the subject, the more silence is required" (p. 223). However, too much silence is also not good. In the end, there is no right answer. You will have to use your judgment. When silence occurs, don't automatically fill it up with words, because then chances are you will say something that you didn't mean to say. And that can quickly cause your tough conversation to become ineffective.

Avoid Emotion

This advice applies to all tough conversations, both personal and professional. There will be times as a school leader when you feel upset when you learn something about your teacher or a staff member. Never ever have the tough conversation during that emotional state. Wait until that emotion is gone—or do a really good job of controlling your emotions during that tough conversation.

Remember That Words Matter

Your choice of words always matters in a tough conversation. Saying things like "I'm disappointed" or "I can't believe you would do something like this" will quickly make the conversation ineffective. Dianna Booher (2017) states, "Strong communicators choose precise words for strategic messages" (p. 76). She explains the importance of avoiding "hot words," or words that you know will likely elicit an emotional response. The best way to choose your words is to always pretend you are being recorded. If others could hear what you are saying, what would their reactions be? Did you say anything that was inappropriate, condescending, or unprofessional?

Use Appropriate Tone

This can be difficult, but you have to know how you sound when you communicate, especially in tough conversations. Sometimes it's a good idea to record yourself and then listen to the tone of your voice. Is your tone abrupt and cold, or is it soft and calm while you are communicating? Sometimes, two people can say the exact same words with completely different perceptions of meaning based on tone of voice. Some school leaders naturally have that soft tone while others do not. If you do not, this is something you can work on to ensure that you are delivering your messages effectively during tough conversations.

Listen

Always listen. Sometimes teachers or staff members have something to say; let them say it. Do not interrupt or talk over them. Let them say their piece. Once they have said what they needed to say, acknowledge it and then go back to your message by reiterating what your expectations are and what they need to do moving forward. Do not let their arguments derail the purpose of your tough conversation. If your tough conversation has gone longer than fifteen minutes, it's probably ineffective.

After the Conversation

Once the tough conversation is over, you can breathe a sigh of relief—you did it! But now, there are some things you should do afterward to ensure the tough conversation was effective. Go back to the purpose of having that conversation in the first place. It was to change a specific behavior, right? You must check to see if that behavior has changed.

Follow Up

Follow up with the teacher or staff member to check in with him or her after the difficult conversation. This is a great time for praise if he or she is now following expectations. Positive compliments and praise will go a long way toward helping the person continue to follow the expectations. This is your indication that the tough conversation was effective. Di Worrall (2013) clarifies:

> Accountability is traditionally viewed as a negative consequence that mandates "punishment" for poor performance . . . a new definition views accountability as a means to produce positive consequences using accountability systems to work together for better results. Celebrating small wins and progress along the way is becoming a tool of choice for progressive leaders. (p. 21)

Think about the positive outcomes of having these tough conversations. This follow-up conversation is where you connect with that particular person. He or she may have left your office upset or angry after the initial tough conversation, but during this follow-up conversation you are shoring up trust by showing this is not personal—you are here to ensure all the adults do what they are supposed to do for the students. And after that tough conversation, when you see that behavior has been corrected, your praise and acknowledgment of that effort will demonstrate that your concern was with the behavior, not the person.

Monitor

You could decide to monitor teachers or staff members (or delegate this responsibility to someone else) for a certain length of time to ensure they are doing what they are supposed to be doing. For instance, if the issue is excessive absences, then keep an eye on the number of absences the teacher takes after you have that tough conversation. Don't just have the talk and assume the behavior will disappear. You will have to monitor it for a while, and when you see improvement, then it's time for the follow-up conversation for the purpose of recognition and praise. Again, highlighting the positive outcomes that resulted from that tough conversation is an effective way to sustain that change.

Summary

The more tough conversations you have, the better you will get at them, and the more effective they'll be. They never stop being difficult, but using the structure of a clear beginning, middle, and end as well as the strategies I outline in this chapter will help you have successful conversations and increase your confidence. Always keep in mind the purpose of every tough conversation you have—to change behavior to better your school for your students.

Reflection Questions

1. What's your biggest barrier to having tough conversations and why? How can you minimize that barrier?

2. Why is it important for school leaders to have those tough conversations?

3. Out of the several tips in this chapter for having tough conversations, which tip will help you the most? Why?

4. Describe a tough conversation you have been avoiding. How would you handle it now?

The School Leader's Communication Challenge: Tough Conversations

The following challenge is designed to be flexible. You can pick one tough conversation that you know you have coming up this month and follow each step closely, or, as you have tough conversations throughout the month, you can use the provided resources to help you reflect and see how they went for you.

Challenge	Notes
• Create your response plan using the reproducible "Our Response to Handbook Violations" (page 81). • Create an agenda using the reproducible "Agenda Template" (page 82) for every tough conversation you have this month. • Document the conversation. • Ensure you follow up with the person after the conversation. • Conduct the SWOT analysis (page 83) and monitor your goal.	

Our Response to Handbook Violations

We expect that every teacher and staff member will adhere to all expectations, policies, and procedures outlined in our faculty handbook. However, occasionally, school administration will respond in the following ways to violations.

Violation	Response
First Time	
Second Time	
Third Time	
Fourth Time	

Connecting Through Leadership © 2020 Solution Tree Press • SolutionTree.com
Visit **go.SolutionTree.com/leadership** to download this free reproducible.

Agenda Template

Purpose of this conversation—What do I want to see happen?

The Structure	My Notes
Beginning • What expectations did the teacher or staff person violate?	
Middle • How has the teacher or staff person violated that expectation? • Provide evidence.	
End • What do you need the teacher or staff person to do moving forward?	

Connecting Through Leadership © 2020 Solution Tree Press • SolutionTree.com
Visit **go.SolutionTree.com/leadership** to download this free reproducible.

SWOT Analysis on My Ability to Have Tough Conversations

Strengths	Weaknesses	Opportunities	Threats
What are you good at when it comes to having tough conversations?	When having tough conversations, what would you consider your weaknesses?	How can you get better at having tough conversations so that it causes the person to change his or her behavior?	Think of the ways tough conversations can go wrong—how can you prevent them?

My goal for future tough conversations:

CHAPTER 4
Communicating Through Writing

Words, once they are printed, have a life of their own.

—Carol Burnett

School leaders write every day. Whether it's writing a quick email or posting a tweet on social media—written communication occurs every day. Because you use this medium so frequently, you must ensure that your writing is effective. In school leadership, your written communication conveys messages to your teachers, parents, students, community members, central office—essentially all your stakeholders. If that message is ineffective or ambiguous, your audience will not receive the message you intend. When you write, you must to confirm that you can say exactly what you want to say, but in writing. Otherwise, ineffective writing skills can lead to confusion, lack of certainty, and perhaps eventually a lack of confidence in your leadership on the part of the people in your organization.

A school leader may use multiple modes of writing—email, text, tweets, and other virtual communication; hard-copy documents; or handwritten notes—and will do so for two different types of audiences, (1) internal and (2) external. The audience for internal written communication comprises people inside the school or district. Communication of this type goes out to teachers, school staff, or central office staff. External written communication, on the other hand, goes to anyone outside the school and district. This audience includes parents, community members, the media, and business partners.

This chapter describes the various ways school leaders communicate in writing and explores strategies to help ensure effective written communication. Specifically, I outline the purpose of written communication, advantages and disadvantages of written communication, and the different types of written communication. I end with reviewing effective strategies for writing and with questions for reflection.

Types of Written Communication

Schools have come a long way from the traditional typed-up memos in mailboxes. Remember walking to the mailroom to check your box for those memos and reading them every day? Now, there are a plethora of options for school leaders when it comes to written communication. You can distribute written communication in a variety of ways. It is important to understand the purpose of your communication before making two important decisions.

1. Can you best meet the purpose of your communication through writing?

2. If yes, what type of written communication will be best to use, and what mode of distribution best suits your purpose?

In the following sections, I discuss the different types of written communication methods to help you decide which type is best for your communication needs.

Emails

Electronic mail has made our lives easier while at the same time introducing new difficulties. How many emails do you think you receive each day? Or even more importantly, how many emails do you send out? The sheer volume of the daily emails can be overwhelming. Knowing how you feel on the receiving end of emails, think about when you should use email as your method of communication. For instance, emails are a great form of written communication for the following situations.

Priority Messaging Regarding Health and Safety

School leaders need to always be proactive when major events occur at school. It's always better to inform your parents of these events right away so there is no time for the parents to receive that information from other sources. For those situations when time is of the essence, email is a great option. For instance, when a fire alarm goes off unexpectedly and you need to let everyone know what happened, you could quickly send out a note like this:

> Dear Faculty and Parents,
>
> We wanted to inform you that a few minutes ago, we had the fire alarm go off. After immediate evacuation and assessment from our local fire department, it was found we have a faulty

smoke alarm in one of our hallways, which will get fixed
tonight. As always, thank you for your support of our school.

Another example of immediate, proactive messaging could be when you need to inform parents of a discipline issue regarding their child (after you unsuccessfully tried to contact them via phone).

Mr. and Mrs. Parent Name,

I tried to call you earlier and did leave a voicemail
but also wanted to follow up in writing to ensure you
receive this message. Unfortunately, we had to suspend
_____ for 2 days because he/she caused a
disruption in his/her classroom. Please call me back at your
earliest convenience so I can share the details of the incident
with you and to discuss our plan moving forward.

Thank you.

Announcements

Emailing is great way to get a message out quickly to a large group of people. In addition to email, there are many other platforms for written communication, and in order to ensure your message gets out the way you intended, sometimes it is a good idea to use a multitude of platforms such as text messaging, the school website, school notification apps, calls during which you read your written message, and so on. Those multiple communication platforms work to get your written words out efficiently and effectively to everyone. Think about all the times a message needs to get out to all our stakeholders at once. An example of this is when there is a change in policy that you want to ensure everyone hears about at the same time:

Dear Faculty and Parents,

Due to the safety and security of all our students, book bags
will no longer be allowed during the school day. When students
come to school, they must put their bags in their lockers—rest
assured that students will receive "locker breaks" during the
school day to go to their lockers to retrieve anything they may
need from their bags. As always, thank you for your support of
our school.

Another example of this is when you need to make an announcement to everyone at the same time, such as when bad weather impacts the operation of your school, as in the following scenario:

> Dear Faculty and Parents,
>
> Due to tomorrow's weather forecast, our school will operate on a two-hour delay. Please see our bell schedule below. As always, thank you for your support.

Documentation

Because emailing is a permanent source of documentation, sometimes the message needs to go into an email. Think about those times when you have given verbal reminders to teachers, but they have not worked. Putting it in writing will help begin that trail of documentation and paperwork that is sometimes necessary to change behaviors, such as the following example:

> Teacher Name,
>
> This is a reminder that per our expectations outlined in the faculty handbook, you need to be at school by 8:30 a.m. If you are unable to get to work by 8:30 a.m., you must notify your administrator.
>
> Thank you.

Emailing is also a great way to summarize the communication in a meeting—because again, the written communication in emails makes them a permanent record for future reference. And there are times when you and your team discuss and share so much in a meeting that you need to make sure you capture it all in writing as a reminder of what everyone agreed to:

> Dear Parent,
>
> Thank you for taking the time to meet with us this morning to discuss the concerns you have had with _____.
> In our meeting, we agreed to the following.
>
> - _____
>
> - _____
>
> I look forward to our follow-up meeting in 6 weeks on
> _____.
>
> Thank you.

Celebrations and Recognitions

Emailing can be a good tool to use when celebrating or recognizing an individual, a group, or the whole school. There are many times when you see something positive happen in your school or something that you know deserves some recognition—a quick email is a great way to capture that moment:

Teacher Name,

It was so nice visiting your classroom today. I was so incredibly
impressed by _____. Thank you for all that you
do for our students and our school.

When Not to Use Email

As you read the examples of the emails in the preceding sections, hopefully you
noticed something. How long is each email? Each sample email is concise—no
more than three sentences. There are two main reasons why conciseness in emails is
important. First, it's the best way to keep the reader's attention—we have all been
in a situation when we receive a long email and we try to scan it for the main ideas
(which could result in us missing some important information). Or we avoid reading
it altogether because of how long it is. Second, it forces the writer to make the email
clear. When you purposefully use the fewest words and sentences possible, you force
yourself to be clear and direct. So when you write an email and you find yourself
typing and typing because you have so much to say, that is a sign that you need to
either pick up the phone and call the person or invite him or her to a meeting. When
you cannot convey your message in three or fewer sentences, email should not be the
form of communication you use in your work as a school leader.

Another instance when emailing is not the best option for written communication
is when you are in an emotional state of mind. Think of those moments when you
have been very upset about something and are about to communicate—while in
that state of mind. An email once sent can never be taken back. When an incident
occurs, or when you get an email from a parent or teacher that makes your blood
boil because you know it was uncalled for or maybe just completely untrue and you
feel the immediate need to defend yourself or your school—don't! At least, not yet.
Communication expert Dawn-Michelle Baude (2007) cautions, "No matter how
angry, insulted, and indignant you are at the email you just received, fight the temp-
tation to let off steam" (p. 16). Calm yourself down and email only when you are no
longer upset or angry.

Finally, never use email to communicate anything that you do not want to go
public. Every time you type up an email, imagine your boss reading it. Imagine the
email being published in the newspaper or being read on the evening news. Imagine
your colleagues reading it. Imagine your parents reading it. You get the point. Every
email you write should be thought of as a public record—because it is. The person
receiving your email is at liberty to forward it to anyone he or she likes—keep that
in mind when writing emails.

Emailing Tips

When you make the decision to communicate in writing through an email, keep in mind the following tips.

Keep It Short and to the Point

How many emails do you get in a day? And how much time do you spend reading through them all? Nobody knows better how time consuming it is to read emails than school leaders. As the school leader, ensure you keep your emails short because as mentioned earlier, you know the people receiving them will probably not read them in their entirety and therefore your message gets lost. Just as with other modes of communication, every email should have a clear beginning, middle, and end (ideally one sentence each). If your email must be lengthy, arrange it in a bulleted or numbered way so it's easier to read, but it's always best to aim for three sentences.

Your beginning sentence is either an acknowledgment of something that has happened or an opening to your message. That first sentence is one sentence—nothing longer. The middle is your second sentence with your message—whatever that message is. If necessary, you can include a bulleted list of reminders or instructions here. For example, look at the second sample email from the Documentation section (page 88)—even though that email is longer than three traditional sentences, look at the second sentence ("In our meeting, we agreed to the following") and note the bullets. The last sentence is your closing.

Answer the Question

When you receive an email and you know you have to respond, answer only the question. There are many times when school leaders receive emails that are filled with anger or disappointment—so when reading through those emails, look for the questions. And then respond by answering the question or the questions. Again, if your answer takes you more than three sentences to respond, then it is better to use a verbal form of communication such as calling that person or having a meeting. After your phone call, it is always a good idea to follow up with a summary of what you discussed in the call in bullet form—that way, you have written documentation of that conversation.

Include a Greeting and Ending

Begin every email by addressing the receiver by name—either by saying "Dear _____" or by referring to the group if the audience is big, such as "Parents" or "Faculty." And every email should have your signature as the sign-off with a "Sincerely" or "Thanks." Some school leaders may use quotes as their signature line;

try using your school's mission statement instead. Your email signature line is a great way to show your branding by publicizing your school's mission.

Use Appropriate Capitalization and Font Size

Remember that capital letters come across as yelling on email, so avoid writing anything in all capital letters. Also avoid using a variety of font types or sizes. Stick to one traditional font type such as Times New Roman and keep the font size traditional. Size 12 often works well.

Include a Subject Line

Always put a subject on the subject line to let the reader know what an email is about. It also makes it easier for your audience to either save, file, or archive that email accordingly so they can find it when they need it.

Edit Before Sending

It's always good practice to read each email over a few times for editing purposes before sending it. Correct any spelling and grammar mistakes, but also cut out as many words as you possibly can. Use the fewest words possible.

Keep It Simple

Choose words carefully in emails. Keep them simple. There is no need to use big words or many words for the sake of sounding professional. For example, consider this email:

> As you are aware, we are endeavoring to implement a novel policy to ensure transition goes smoothly and effortlessly sans major issues transpiring. Therefore, beginning next week, we are asking that we all adhere to the new procedures that were previously communicated with you at our grade-level meetings.

Now consider this email:

> Beginning next week, we will implement the new transition procedures that were shared with you at the grade-level meetings.

In fact, Kenneth Roman and Joel Raphaelson (2000) state that the editors at *The Wall Street Journal* have "put into practice this simple principle: Short sentences and short paragraphs are easier to read than long ones. And easier to understand" (p. 10). The authors share examples of which words you should avoid and which ones to use instead (table 4.1, page 92).

Table 4.1: Words to Avoid and Use

Avoid	Use
Currently	Now
Initiate	Start
Indicate	Show
Utilize	Use
At this point in time	Now
With regard to	About
Despite the fact that	Although
Hold a meeting	Meet
Due to the fact that	Because

Letters and Cards

Letters and cards are another form of written communication. Although you likely to do not use letters and cards as frequently as emails, it is still a valid form of written communication. School leaders typically write letters for a couple of reasons: (1) to express a concern or (2) to provide information. Letters should always appear on the school or district's letterhead stationery and should always include the school or district's full address and phone number. Handwritten cards, on the other hand, can be cards that the school purchases or perhaps makes using school or district colors or mascots. People always appreciate handwritten cards—they seem more personal than an email. School leaders typically write cards for a few reasons, such as to recognize or acknowledge someone, to thank someone, or to check up on someone.

Letter for Expressing Concern

There are times when you might need to give a formal letter to a staff member because of performance issues or to parents to warn them their child is struggling academically or behaviorally. What makes a letter different from an email is that the letter is more formal—whereas the teacher or parent may interpret an email as a friendly reminder to do something:

> In today's busy society, the mere fact that someone has taken the time to sit down and draft a letter rather than make a telephone call may indicate that the writer sees the issue as of greater importance. Couple that with corporate letterhead, and suddenly the impact has increased dramatically. (Muckian & Woods, 1996, p. 16)

Letters highlight the importance of content, for instance, the importance of the receiver changing a particular behavior. If the behavior doesn't change, these types of letters can also be used for evidence as "they effectively establish the paper trail that lawyers and judges so dearly cherish" (Muckian & Woods, 1996, p. 16).

The letter of concern should always come after you have already had a face-to-face conversation or sent a gentle email reminder. The letter is longer than three lines because it needs to capture nuances of the issues you have been having with the staff person and clearly explain the directives moving forward. Again, like most communication methods, this letter needs a beginning, middle, and end. The beginning outlines what the purpose of the letter is. The middle is your case—the bullet points that illustrate what the problem is. The end is your paragraph outlining what your directives are moving forward and what could possibly happen if they are not met. Throughout the entire letter, you are only discussing facts. The reproducible "Sample Letter of Concern Template" (page 105) includes a template that follows this format, in addition to a letter example.

Letter for Providing Information

Sometimes you might write a letter to just provide information to stakeholders. Maybe you provide one during an open house to outline the exciting events happening in the new school year, or maybe you send welcome-back letters after the summer. There could be follow-up letters to parents after a discipline was assigned to their children or academic letters to parents about their children's academic placement. Letters can also impart information to businesses when they become partners with your school; you can use the letter to outline what that partnership will look like. In essence, letters are a formal way to communicate information about your school, information about events happening, or disciplinary or academic developments. The reproducible "Sample Informational Letter Template" (page 107) includes some sample letter templates that you can use to provide information to stakeholders and sample letters.

Card for Recognition or Acknowledgment

You can write cards to recognize or acknowledge teachers, staff, students, parents, or business partners. These are quick handwritten notes to acknowledge a job well done or perhaps a significant event such as a wedding or a birthday. I encourage you to take the time to write these cards to recognize behaviors you want to see repeated in your school. Acknowledgment, taking time to recognize significant moments, helps build connections and relationships. "We've gotten away from the practice of sending personal, handwritten notes and letters of congratulations . . . so if you send one, yours may make a lasting impression" (Lamb, 2011, p. 28). Recognition and acknowledgment will always go a long way.

Thank-You Card

Cards are always a great way to thank your teachers, staff members, and parents for going above and beyond for you or your school or doing something extraordinary, such as staying after school to help out with a project or volunteering to stay late for an extracurricular activity. For the same reasons I've previously stated, take the time to send a handwritten thank-you card.

Card for Checking Up

Life happens all the time in schools. There are almost always people going through a tough time during the course of the school year, like the loss of a family member or a medical issue. Depending on the situation, a handwritten card to check up on them and let them know you are there for them may really make a difference and allow you to build and strengthen your connections.

Social Media

Social media is a great platform for written communication for school leaders—especially when you are looking for a one-way mode of communication to push information out quickly and efficiently without expecting a response back. Keeping in mind how much technology has changed, and how every new generation that comes into your school is most likely very well versed in social media, you are missing out on a huge audience if you choose to ignore social media as a medium for communication. Social media expert Andrea Williams (2017) states, "Leaders must get comfortable on social media if they want to engage in successful internal communications with their employees and successful external communications with their customers." In schools, your customers include all your stakeholders. However, once you decide you will use social media for written communication, Booher (2017) recommends selecting one or two social media platforms that you will use to communicate messages. Then, stay consistent with the messages you post.

Twitter

One of the great things about Twitter is that it forces you to keep your message short. Twitter is a great tool to communicate reminders like the following:

> Remember we have our concert coming up tomorrow evening at 6:00. Please be sure to park in the back parking lot. We look forward to seeing our kids perform!

Twitter is one of the best ways to get positive information out there about your school. You can post pictures and comments about all the fantastic things happening at your school—a great activity students are working on or teachers participating in a team-building activity or parents hosting an event for other parents—anything going on in your school is worth putting up on Twitter to publicize the great events that occur on a daily basis under your leadership.

Blogs

Some school leaders use blogs to communicate with their teachers and parents. Blogs work well if you publish entries consistently, such as every Sunday or Monday, because this way the audience knows to expect it. The weekly blog is a good way to minimize emails. You can keep track of all those announcements or reminders that come up during the week, but instead of sending out emails all the time, put it all into the weekly blog. It helps streamline the communication because your staff and parents will know that you will post everything they need to know for that week in the blog. You can organize the blog in the following structure.

- Calendar for the Week
  › This outlines all the events coming up during the week.
- Announcements
  › This section contains announcements or reminders that the audience of this blog needs to be aware of.
- Recognitions and Celebrations
  › This part highlights any celebrations or recognitions from the previous week.

No matter whom you write the blog for—your staff or your parents—keep it consistent and updated and, when writing the blog, organize it into sections. Some school leaders may combine the blogs, but keep in mind the information you want to send to your staff could be different from what you want to send out to parents. However, the blog for parents can be for both teachers and parents because your staff should know what communication goes out to the parents.

Website

It is common for schools to have websites. But remember, if the website is not effective, it's almost better for your school not to have one (which I do not recommend). Take the time to figure out what components you want on your school's website—and then how you want them organized and displayed. What are all the headers you want to use? Following are some examples of items that could be of value to include on your website.

- School information
- Administration information
- Faculty information

- Strategic plan
- Calendar
- Clubs and sports
- Curriculum information
- Current school announcements (for example, a link to the weekly newsletter)

Pamela DeLoatch (2015) explores what makes websites effective, using the same criteria that the Web Marketing Association uses when it determines which websites on the internet are the best. Those specific attributes include the following.

- Design (color, text, visuals, and so on)
- Innovation (original layout or standard website templates)
- Content (relevant, updated regularly, and so on)
- Technology (pages get uploaded quickly, hyperlinks all work, and so on)
- Interactivity (includes texts, videos, pictures, hyperlinks, and so on)
- Ease of use (easy to figure out where everything is)
- Mobile friendly (can be used from a mobile device such as a smartphone)

It sometimes helps to get your stakeholders' input on what kind of information they want to see on your website; ultimately, they are the ones who will visit it and read it so you should cater to their needs. See the reproducible "Sample Survey" (page 109) for a sample survey to solicit feedback for your school's website.

Newsletters

Newsletters can be another valuable tool for written communication. School leaders typically intend them for all stakeholders: parents, teachers, students, and so on. They appear consistently either every week or every month and contain valuable information about what is happening at the school. It is a structured and organized way to communicate pertinent information that stakeholders need to know.

Keeping this information relevant can sometimes become a concern. A newsletter should not become so long that people no longer read it. Think about how you want to structure your newsletter. For instance, the first page should always be the principal's page. This space is for the principal to make his or her announcements, reminders, and so on. You can reserve the second page for recognition for students and staff. The third page can be for any school club announcements. The fourth page can be the PTA's page where the parent leaders in your school can communicate their information. From that point on, the newsletter can have a variety of community and business partner advertisements. Newsletters can be either in hard copy (if your school has the funds to make that many copies) or electronic, which you can email as well as post on the school's website. Some schools leave a few printed copies at the front desk for parents and other visitors to read while they are waiting to be helped.

The key to a successful school newsletter is to have a consistent structure so your stakeholders know where information is. Another strategy is to collaborate with your PTA, foundation, or any other parent leadership group, and with club sponsors and sports teams, to ensure the school publishes one newsletter containing all school-relevant information. Less effective are multiple newsletters from different people.

Handbooks or Manuals

Many times, school leaders will publish handbooks or manuals that provide the school's procedures or processes on how to do something. Examples can include the faculty handbook or a handbook regarding a specific process such as a professional learning community (PLC) or positive behavioral interventions and supports (PBIS). Handbooks are an excellent way to clearly communicate those expectations to your staff. Jerome Forde (2017) points out, "A handbook also creates a level playing field among the employees themselves. Written policies demonstrate to everyone they are being treated fairly and equally."

If you have clearly communicated your expectations in writing, in some kind of a handbook, it makes it easier for teachers to do what you expect of them because they know. Not knowing can lead to confusion or different interpretations of expectations depending on what each person hears versus having it all clearly written down. Therefore, handbooks and manuals can also be a preventive measure. Forde (2017) states, "The biggest benefit of an employee handbook is undoubtedly the fact that it mitigates the risk of employee misconduct and discontent."

Ultimately, you want your staff to do what you expect. It becomes your responsibility then to ensure that communication is clear—and in writing where it is permanent and where your teachers and staff can refer to it whenever they need. Following is a list of topics that you could include in a school's handbook.

- Mission, vision, values, and goals
- Administration and staff names
- Leadership team names and roles
- Communication expectations
- Instructional expectations
- Meeting expectations
- Supervision expectations
- Attendance policies
- Student discipline procedures

- Budget
- Safety procedures

With all the different forums that you can use to communicate, it is very beneficial to create a schoolwide communication plan. It is important to put the communication plan in writing. You can do this collaboratively with a variety of your stakeholders. See the reproducible "Sample Communication Plan Template" (page 110).

Purpose of Written Communication

As with any kind of communication (verbal or written), you must first determine your purpose. What are the various reasons to communicate in writing?

- Disseminating, summarizing, or clarifying information
- Praising or recognizing individuals or groups
- Reminding others about tasks or deadlines
- Asking questions
- Requesting feedback
- Relaying procedures or rules
- Announcing events

It is important to be able to answer the question, What is the reason for my writing? But the following question is even more important: Why am I choosing to write instead of talk? The next section outlines advantages and disadvantages of choosing written communication to help you answer that question.

Advantages and Disadvantages of Written Communication

There are advantages and disadvantages of written communication. Once you know the purpose for your communication, you can use this list to see if putting that communication in writing will help or hinder it. It will help you determine if the message you want to communicate is best communicated in writing or verbally.

Advantages of Written Communication

Sometimes putting something in writing really is the best way. These advantages are well worth considering before picking up the phone or setting up a meeting.

Provides Permanent Documentation

A great advantage of written communication is that it is permanent. It will always be there for you to refer to, and you can save it for as long as you need it. When your stakeholders forget something or need a reminder, that written communication is always there for you to show them, whereas with verbal communication, sometimes there is no proof of what you said. The words are lost as soon as they come out of your mouth. There is no going back five years later to see what you said—but you can find what you wrote.

Improves Accuracy

With the written word, you have a higher chance of ensuring that you communicate accurate information, since you have the time to review your words. You can write and then rewrite until you get exactly what you want before publishing what you've written. With verbal communication, if people do not understand your message, you have to repeat it in a different way, and that could be difficult to do if you are on the spot.

Allows for Input

You can solicit input and feedback for your written communication before publishing it. You have the time to show it to another colleague or someone from your leadership team or even your supervisor to ensure that you are conveying the message you are trying to convey. With verbal communication, however, you can prepare for it ahead of time, but once you are speaking, you are on your own.

Decreases Confusion or Misinterpretation

With effective written communication, you decrease the likelihood of people misinterpreting your message, because everyone gets the same message at the same time when you publish your written communication. Also, you have more time to anticipate the possible ways your words could be misinterpreted and correct those problems before they happen. With verbal communication, people can distort what you say. Or what you say may not get repeated the same way to others who did not actually hear what you said.

Is Efficient for One-Way Communication

Written communication is more efficient if you have to send a message out to a large group or to multiple stakeholders (one-way communication). Verbal communication, on the other hand, means you either individually call each person or set up a face-to-face meeting with each person, which can be time consuming. Of course, a presentation is another form of verbal communication that could also serve to disseminate information. As a leader, you need to decide which information will be better communicated in person via a presentation or through writing.

Disadvantages of Written Communication

Before you start shooting off emails or writing up memos, it's important to remember that although it has many advantages, written communication can also create issues in some situations.

Creates a Public Record

One of the downsides of written communication is that it is very public. Even if you send something in writing to one person, that one person can send it to anyone else or show it to anyone else. You can keep verbal communication between you and the other person or persons—even if they tell someone else what you said, there is no evidence that that is what you actually said (unless of course they recorded it).

Is Inefficient for Two-Way Communication

Written communication can be a slow process if the communication is two-sided. In other words, when you are writing to someone or a group of people, you have to wait until they read it, and then you have to wait for their responses. With verbal communication, however, you will be able to have that two-way communication much more quickly and therefore reach the purpose of that communication.

Can Lack Conciseness or Clarity

One disadvantage of written communication is that it may lack focus or clarity. When the written message is too verbose or convoluted, it loses its meaning. People may just stop reading your messages because they know how time consuming it is to read through all those words and try to decipher what exactly you are trying to say. Verbal communication can be effective only if you are able to speak concisely and clearly. If you are verbose both verbally and in writing, then you will have a problem.

Can Be Impersonal

Written communication is not the best way to build or strengthen relationships. When your stakeholders receive something in writing, it has the potential to be less personal when compared to a face-to-face verbal message. For example, because written communication is so permanent and can be seen as documentation, it should always be formal and to the point—making it feel impersonal.

Can Lack Sensitivity

Written communication is also not great for communicating sensitive information. For instance, if there is a tragic event in your school such as a death of a faculty member or student, an email would not be the best mode of communication for that information. It can be difficult to capture sensitive emotions and feelings through written communication.

Has Legal Implications

A big disadvantage of written communication is the possibility that everything you write can be used against you. Lawyers or media personnel can take one sentence out of context or misinterpret your written message. Teachers can take what you write and file grievances against you if you wrote something that could be perceived as a violation of a board rule or policy.

Elements of Effective Written Communication

Michelle Brooks (2017) outlines several reasons why it is so important to master the art of written communication.

- **Getting your message across:** If you write well, others will receive the message that you are trying to communicate in the way you want them to. Everything you write should serve a purpose; effective writing ensures you meet it.

- **Demonstrating intelligence:** Effective writing demonstrates your intelligence level. Your ability to organize your thoughts in a clear, concise manner that is free of errors and confusion demonstrates not only your ability to write well, but your ability to communicate strongly as a leader. Think about written messages you have received that are filled with errors or written in a way that poorly communicates the message. It makes you think differently about the writer compared to someone who writes a clear, concise message.

- **Keeping good records:** Effective writing allows you to maintain good records as everything you write will always be there. If your written communication has been effective, your records will accurately reflect actual events.

You know why good writing skills are essential to leadership, so no matter what form you use for written communication, it's important to keep in mind some basic tips to ensure your writing is effective and therefore fulfills its purpose. I discuss each tip in detail in the following sections.

Use Clear Verbiage

Use words that are easy to understand. When school leaders start using unnecessarily complex words or repeating themselves, they convolute their message. This means the message is now difficult to understand. Professional communicator Frank J. Pietrucha (2014) asserts, "It is your responsibility to make sure that your text is as effortless as possible for your reader. This means removing any roadblocks that slow down a fluid exchange of ideas" (p. 103).

Edit for Correctness and Clarity

Please ensure you use correct spelling and grammar. As a school leader, people look up to you and expect that you put time and effort into your written communication so that it does not go out filled with various errors. It is your responsibility to check to ensure you do not make mistakes. Otherwise, the message of your written communication may get lost as your readers focus on the errors. In addition, Pietrucha (2014) recommends critically questioning your content: "Are you using big words unnecessarily? Are your web pages filled with jargon? Are your sentences and paragraphs too long?" (p. 103).

Be Professional

Just like others would expect you to be professional during meetings or a presentation, your written communication requires that same level of professionalism. Everything you write should always be written in a professional tone. Stay away from jokes, sarcasm, or anything that others could see as unprofessional.

Know Your Audience

Although your writing should always be professional (because it is subject to open records), you may tailor the writing to the audience. For instance, if you are writing to parents, you may need to spell out the acronyms and education language that only your teachers would understand.

Keep to Your Purpose

Always go back to the purpose of your communication. After you have written your message, using whichever method you selected, ask yourself whether it serves that purpose. Probably one of the most important things you can do is to ensure your written communication serves its purpose.

Summary

Because you write every day, it is one of your primary modes of communicating and getting your message across to your audience. It becomes imperative then that your written communication is strong. Take the time to know the purpose of your written message, plan your message, and remember to always take the time to edit, edit, edit.

Reflection Questions ↩

1. Describe how you can incorporate three of the tips for effective writing from this chapter into your writing.

2. For what purpose do you write the most? How can you ensure you meet that purpose every time you write?

3. Review some emails you have written recently. How could you have written them differently to make them clearer and more concise? Be sure to look at the length and the unnecessary words you may have used.

4. Analyze your faculty handbook. How can you bring more clarity to it to ensure you have clearly communicated expectations to the staff?

The School Leader's Communication Challenge: Writing

The following challenge is designed to be flexible. Depending on your needs and upcoming schedule, you can pick one important email, letter, or other written communication you know you will send this month and follow each step closely, or you can use the provided resources to help you reflect on all the writing you do this month.

Challenge	Notes
• Create an updated faculty handbook with all your expectations clearly communicated in writing. • Ensure every written communication has simple, easy-to-understand verbiage (see the reproducibles on pages 105–109 for some sample pieces). • Create your communication plan using the reproducible "Sample Communication Plan Template" (page 110). • Conduct the SWOT analysis (page 111) and monitor your goal.	

Connecting Through Leadership © 2020 Solution Tree Press • SolutionTree.com
Visit **go.SolutionTree.com/leadership** to download this free reproducible.

Sample Letter of Concern Template

Beginning: State the purpose of the letter.

"The purpose of this letter is to serve as a letter of direction regarding our expectations of your future job performance. This letter will summarize the meeting we had on *insert date*."

Middle: State the issues and provide your evidence.

"On *insert date, insert name of who else was with you in the meeting* and I met with you to discuss the following concerns.

- *Insert concern*

- *Insert concern*

- *Insert concern.*"

End: Reiterate your expectations moving forward, and what can happen if those expectations are not met (each of these directives should correlate to the concern you have).

"Moving forward, you are expected to adhere to the policies and procedures outlined in the faculty handbook. Specifically, you are directed to:

- *Insert directive*

- *Insert directive*

- *Insert directive*

Failure to comply with these directives could result in further disciplinary action."

Sample Letter of Concern

The purpose of this letter is to serve as a letter of direction regarding our expectations for your future job performance. This letter will summarize the meeting we had on November 6.

On November 6, Assistant Principal John Doe and I met with you to discuss the following concerns.

- You are inputting several grades for your unit into your gradebook a day before grades are due for report cards.

- You missed the last four help sessions for your students.

- You have been absent from your duty post over the last couple of weeks.

Connecting Through Leadership © 2020 Solution Tree Press • SolutionTree.com
Visit **go.SolutionTree.com/leadership** to download this free reproducible.

Moving forward, you are expected to adhere to the policies and procedures outlined in the faculty handbook. Specifically, you are directed to do the following.

- Input your grades into your gradebook in a timely manner—specifically, three days after the assignment is turned in (page 23 in the faculty handbook—under grading expectations).

- Present at all your help sessions for students. If an emergency comes up, notify your administrator that you are unable to attend (page 16 in the faculty handbook—under teacher help session expectations).

- Be present at your duty station. If an emergency comes up, notify your administrator that you are unable to be at your duty station (page 17 in the faculty handbook—under teacher supervision expectations).

Failure to comply with these directives may result in further disciplinary action.

Thank you.

Connecting Through Leadership © 2020 Solution Tree Press • SolutionTree.com
Visit **go.SolutionTree.com/leadership** to download this free reproducible.

Sample Informational Letter Template

Beginning: Introduce what this letter will be about.

Middle: Provide the actual information.

End: Close with a thank you.

Sample Informational Letter:

Letter to Parents of Students With Multiple Discipline Referrals

Dear Parents,

As we end the year, we have several activities planned for our students, but we want to remind all our students that these are privileges. With that in mind, we pulled a report to show students who have accumulated three or more office referrals this school year, and your child's name was on this report. We want to maximize the time your child spends in class, so we will be implementing alternative discipline measures for any future discipline code violations after spring break.

Beginning Monday, April 15, if your child is written up for an infraction that would typically result in an in-school suspension, your child instead will lose one of the following privileges, depending on his or her grade level.

Sixth Grade	Seventh Grade	Eighth Grade
Intramurals	Intramurals	Intramurals
Olympics	Olympics	Olympics
Yearbook Signing Party	Yearbook Signing Party	Yearbook Signing Party
End-of-Year Celebration	End-of-Year Celebration	Eighth-Grade Dance
		Orlando Trip (Music Students)

If your child violates a discipline code that would result in out-of-school suspension, then he or she will still receive the out-of-school suspension in addition to losing one of the privileges.

We met with your child this week, and he or she has been made aware of future consequences for any referrals received after spring break.

Page 1 of 2

Connecting Through Leadership © 2020 Solution Tree Press • SolutionTree.com
Visit **go.SolutionTree.com/leadership** to download this free reproducible.

Hopefully, this will help motivate your child and deter him or her from violating our discipline policies and codes during the last six weeks of school as we know many students want to participate in the year-end activities.

As always, we appreciate your support.

Sample Informational Letter:

Welcome Back Letter to Parents After Summer

Dear Parents,

Hopefully everyone is enjoying the summer and staying cool in this heat! Yes, this yearly summer letter does mean the opening of school is not too far away. I wanted to thank all of you for a wonderful school year. We had some great accomplishments!

As many of you are aware, one of our strategic plan goals for the upcoming school year was to increase the percentage of students who score in the exceeding category on the state assessments. The increase was achieved in sixth-grade social studies, mathematics, and science; seventh-grade social studies, science, and language arts; and eighth-grade social studies and writing. I have attached our test scores for the past three years for your review with this letter.

In addition to our test scores, following are just a few of the successes from this past school year.

- Established our vision and mission
- Implemented common assessments to ensure all students are assessed the same
- Implemented ways to celebrate and honor students, including a weekly newsletter and eighth-grade ceremony
- Syllabus outlining consistent practices throughout each content area
- Redesigned our website
- Restructured teaching assignments, teams, and classrooms

As we start this school year, we value your feedback. Please take a few minutes to answer two questions: (1) What did we do well? and (2) What do we need to work on? Thank you in advance for your input! We look forward to another great school year!

Sample Survey

We'd like feedback on our new website design. Please answer the following questions.

1. What purpose should our website serve?

2. What feature do you use the most on our website?

3. What features would you like to see added on our website?

4. What aspects of our website do you like?

5. What information is missing on our website?

6. What information is unnecessary on our website?

7. What information is hard to access on our website?

8. What kinds of images would you like to see on our website?

9. What part of our website would you most like to see improved?

10. Overall, how satisfied are you with our current school website?

REPRODUCIBLE

Sample Communication Plan Template

Mode of Communication	Audience	Frequency	Person Responsible

Connecting Through Leadership © 2020 Solution Tree Press • SolutionTree.com
Visit **go.SolutionTree.com/leadership** to download this free reproducible.

SWOT Analysis on My Writing Skills

Strengths	Weaknesses	Opportunities	Threats
What are you good at when it comes to writing?	When writing, what would you consider your weaknesses?	How can you get better at writing so that your writing serves the purpose you intend?	Think of ways your writing could be misinterpreted—how can you prevent them?

My goal for improving my writing skills:

CHAPTER 5

Communicating Through Body Language

Nonverbal communication is an elaborate secret code that is written nowhere, known by none, and understood by all.

—Edward Sapir

When we think about communication, oral and written are usually the two modes we think about. But communication through body language is another very important and impactful method of communication. You can communicate many messages through the way you look at people, the way you sit, the way you use your hands, the way you stand, and so on.

As a school leader, you owe it to your school to understand how your body language communicates messages to your students, teachers, parents, and other stakeholders, including those who are from cultures other than yours. You may be saying one thing, but your body language may be saying something completely different. Therefore, it is important to be aware of your body language so that it aligns with what you are communicating verbally (in a meeting, a presentation, or a tough conversation). You could put hours and hours of time into preparing for a meeting only for your body language to make it ineffective. Or you could spend hours preparing for a tough conversation and say all the right words, but your body language could completely undo that conversation. And the worst part is, you may never realize it was your body language that hindered your message.

Let's define exactly what *body language* is as it relates to communication: "Body language describes the method of communicating using body movements or gestures instead of, or in addition to, verbal language" (Patel, 2014, p. 90). Your body can speak for you even when you are not saying anything. Think about how your body language can communicate certain messages to your stakeholders when you're listening to them speak. And of course, on the other hand, your body language can communicate even while you are communicating with words. The challenge is that you may not be aware that you are communicating through movements or gestures. This can easily give rise to inconsistent messages. These "mixed messages create tension and distrust because the receiver senses that the communicator is hiding something or is being less than candid" (Wertheim, n.d., p. 2).

Much of this book revolves around how we communicate using words, either face to face or through writing. But Robert W. Kaps and John K. Voges (2007) argue that "communication has more to do with the way we look, how we convey a message, and the way we say things, rather than the actual verbal message" (p. 43). This does not diminish the importance of communicating through the spoken and written word, but it does highlight the value of keeping all forms of communication in mind and ensuring they work in concert. That is why this chapter in a book about communication is so necessary: because it's not something many school leaders are cognizant of and yet it can make such an impact on their messages. Simply put:

> We communicate as many messages nonverbally as we do
> verbally. Nonverbal communication—the way we stand, the
> distance we maintain from another person, the way we walk,
> the way we fold our arms and wrinkle our brow, our eye
> contact, being late for a meeting—conveys messages to others.
> (Lunenburg, 2010, p. 1)

This chapter explores the impact body language has on communication and what body language can communicate to your staff and stakeholders. I outline the three main sources of body language: (1) face, (2) arms and hands, and (3) legs and feet. I then share how your appearance plays a role in body language as well as how emotional intelligence can improve your body language. Finally, I provide tips for leaders on body language before concluding the reflection questions.

Impact of Body Language Communication

Because body language is also a form of communication—one that you may not necessarily be aware of—it is important to understand the impact it can have on your communication. In fact, Edward G. Wertheim (n.d.) argues, "A large percentage . . .

of the meaning we derive from communication, we derive from the non-verbal cues that the other person gives" (p. 2). With that said, body language is clearly important when discussing communication. Wertheim (n.d.) outlines five reasons why body language is so important.

1. Repetition

2. Contradiction

3. Substitution

4. Complementing

5. Accenting

Repetition

You can use body language to repeat the message that you are communicating in words. You can say something, and your body language (whether ot not you realize it) reiterates what you say. Think about talking during a presentation where you are providing professional development to your staff. You are about to begin an activity that will require teachers to go stand on either side of the room. As you are telling them this, you are also using your hands to direct them to which side they need to stand on. Your use of body language is repeating the message you are communicating verbally.

Contradiction

On the other hand, sometimes your body language can say the opposite of what your words are saying. When your body language is contradicting what your words are saying, that implies to others that what you are saying isn't true. For example, imagine you are meeting with a group of teachers to tell them a new platform to input teacher absences is about to be implemented in your district. You are telling them this new platform is going to make it so much easier to enter your absences, but while you are telling them this, you roll your eyes. Immediately, your teachers no longer believe you because your body language does not support your verbal message.

Substitution

When you use body language instead of words, it's called substitution. You are substituting this nonverbal form of communication for more obvious verbal forms. For instance, you are meeting with parents and their student because the student has been disrupting the classroom. You want the student to tell the parents what he or she has been doing, so you look at him or her and tilt your head and raise your eyebrows. That body language is signaling the student to speak—and you do this without saying a word. Or it can be less subtle: your secretary comes into your office to ask if the decorations in the conference room look good, and you respond by giving her a thumbs-up. Again, your body language communicated the message without you having to use words.

Complementing

You can also use body language to emphasize the message that you communicate with words. In this case, you are using body language to match your words. This of course is a great way to use body language because you are confirming your message to your audience. For example, you give positive feedback to a teacher after observing his or her classroom, and you smile and give him or her a quick round of applause. Your body language in this case is supporting your verbal message, therefore complementing it. Although complementing can be similar to repetition in many ways, with complementing, you are using body language to emphasize and support the message that you are communicating with words, while with repetition your gestures directly repeat the message you are conveying with words.

Accenting

Accenting is very similar to complementing and repetition. When using your body language to accent your verbal message, you are really trying to ensure that others receive your message. It can also show the emotion behind the message. For instance, if you are announcing to your staff or parents that the school just received an award, your body language during this announcement could involve you applauding, smiling, and maybe even jumping up and down. That body language is not just complementing your message but accenting your message. You are intentionally using your body language to emphasize your verbal message.

What Body Language Can Communicate

As with any type of communication, body language offers several purposes that leaders should be aware of. Specifically, Silvia Bonaccio, Jane O'Reilly, Sharon L. O'Sullivan, and François Chiocchio (2016) outline five functions that body language can communicate.

1. Demonstrate personal qualities.
2. Establish hierarchy.
3. Promote social functioning.
4. Foster high-quality relationships.
5. Display emotions.

Demonstrate Personal Qualities

Body language can communicate a lot about your personality or attitude. Think about every time you interview candidates for your school—their body language from the minute they walk into your office communicates a lot about their personality or attitude. Now think of your own body language. How does it communicate your attitude or personality to your staff or stakeholders? If someone is arrogant, he or she could communicate that via body language by swaggering into your office and sitting down without waiting to be invited. On the other hand, if someone is insecure or shy, he or she may display completely different communication through body language, such as avoiding eye contact or not smiling.

Establish Hierarchy

Body language can establish your position in a hierarchy. You're the leader in the building, and your body language needs to communicate that. Think of how you stand and how you sit; even these simple, nonverbal behaviors communicate that you are the leader in your school (or not). Carol Kinsey Goman (2018) states, "Great leaders sit, stand, walk, and gesture in ways that exude confidence, competence, and status." As an example, in her book *The Silent Language of Leaders*, Goman (2011b) references research conducted at Harvard Business School that discusses high-power poses as they relate to standing. For instance, standing with legs and arms spread exudes that confidence because you're indicating without words that you do not feel vulnerable. You will see more specific examples of body language poses later in this chapter.

Promote Social Functioning

Body language can help build relationships not just at your school but outside your school as well. Think about it—people are more likely want to be around you if your body language communicates you are approachable, enthusiastic, and positive.

Foster High-Quality Relationships

Bonaccio et al. (2016) state that in addition to social functioning, body language can build long-term relationships that are committed and based on trust. They discuss the concept of rapport—you as a school leader know it is essential to have rapport with your staff and stakeholders. You can build rapport through trust, which you in turn can build through body language. With trust being established or strengthened through body language, think about all the ways you can use this to connect with your stakeholders. Reporter Ruth Umoh (2018) provides a few tips (we will explore many of these later in the chapter as well).

- **Tilt your head:** It shows a willingness to be vulnerable and therefore connect with the person you are communicating with.

- **Maintain appropriate eye contact:** Looking stakeholders in the eye (but not too much) shows you are sincere and builds trust.

- **Open your palms:** Keeping your palms opens show you are trustworthy and credible, again helping you connect with your audience.

- **Use a glove handshake:** This term refers to when you shake someone's hand but then place your other hand on top gently; this communicates kindness and trustworthiness.

- **Be a mirror:** Mirroring other people's body language can help build trust, which again will help you connect with them.

Display Emotions

Finally, body language communicates your emotions. Your face and gestures communicate how you are feeling—which can be great if you are excited and want your staff, parents, and students to know about it. But as a leader, it's not so great if you are frustrated or angry.

Face

You may or may not be aware of what your face does while you are speaking. This section breaks down some of the different ways you communicate using your face.

Eye Contact

Your eyes can say a lot. Squinting your eyes when you don't understand something or opening them wide because you are shocked—both can communicate a message. Eye contact or lack of eye contact also communicates messages. For example, if you don't make eye contact when you are meeting with someone in your office, it could communicate lack of interest. On the other hand, eye contact with a person you are talking with could communicate you are intrigued by what he or she is saying. Closing your eyes for longer periods than a blink can signal you are trying to keep out all the noise and distractors so you can focus.

Head

Think about the head movements you make when you are communicating verbally. A very common head movement is the nod. You do this every day, but have you ever thought of how you can use it? When you are nodding, what message are you sending to your audience? Or when you shake your head, what message does that send? You can convey disappointment or a simple answer of no by shaking your head. Tilting your head is another way to send a nonverbal message—perhaps of confusion. Either way, the movement of your head communicates a message.

Facial Expressions

If you think about all the muscles that control your face, from the mouth to the lips to the eyes and forehead, it is no wonder that researchers state we produce thousands of facial expressions (Ekman, 1977). In his research, Paul Ekman (1977) identifies forty-two muscles in the face that are responsible for making expressions—which can produce over ten thousand configurations. Specifically, three thousand of those relate to emotions. In addition, Ekman (1977) discovered (after decades of research and experiments) that among those three thousand facial expressions that express emotions, there are six universal facial expressions that all people interpret the same way—no matter their cultural background. Those facial expressions are happiness, sadness, surprise, fear, anger, and disgust. So, think about what your facial expressions look like when you are feeling any of these emotions. Chances are, no matter what words are coming out of your mouth, your staff and stakeholders will know how you really feel if they are able to interpret your facial expressions.

Smiles

Although smiling is a facial expression, it needs its own section. Whether the smile is genuine or fake, smiling will almost always convey a positive message to your staff and stakeholders. Goman (2018) asserts, "Smiling is a positive signal that is under-used by leaders. A smile is an invitation, a sign of welcome and inclusion. It says, 'I'm friendly and approachable.'"

In addition, smiles are infectious:

> Whether we realize it or not, we automatically copy the facial expressions we see. This is why regular smiling is important to have as a part of your body-language repertoire, even when you don't feel like it, because smiling directly influences other people's attitudes and how they respond to you. (Pease & Pease, 2006, p. 71)

So think about the impact smiling can have when you are building trust and connecting with your stakeholders. Smiling can be a powerful type of body language to communicate many positive messages, all of which will help you connect with your audience.

Hands and Arms

Think about all the times you use your hands and arms when communicating. Again, just like with your face, you may or may not even be aware of the messages you are communicating using your hands and arms. Let's begin with the hands.

Hands

A very common form of body language communication is the handshake. There are so many messages that you can communicate through a handshake. Goman (2011a) provides several tips to ensure the message that you communicate through your handshake is that of sincerity.

- When shaking hands, make eye contact.

- Smile.

- Stand when extending your hand.

- Offer your hand with your palm facing sideways (instead of it facing upward or downward).

- Shake hands firmly.

- With the other hand, touch the other person's elbow.

- Start talking before you let go.

- When you break away, don't look down.

In addition to the handshake, think of other nonverbal behaviors you engage in using your hands. Consultant Nicolas Fradet (n.d.) describes the different hand gestures we use and what they could mean.

- **Palms up:** When you hold your arms out with your palms facing up, that usually shows openness and trustworthiness. Others see this type of body language as positive.

- **Palms down:** On the other hand, when you hold your arms out with the palms facing down, you are showing your authority and that you are in command of the situation.

- **Hands on the heart:** This communicates that you want your staff and stakeholders to trust you or believe you.

- **Chopping movements:** When you use your hands to make chopping movements, you are communicating that what you are saying is absolutely certain and it will not change.

- **Finger pointing:** People typically see pointing a finger at anyone as impolite and perhaps even confrontational or aggressive.

- **Squeezing hands or knuckle cracking:** Fidgeting or playing with your hands can communicate your nervousness or your uncertainty.

- **Hands in pockets:** This can communicate your lack of interest in the person you are communicating with or that you do not trust him or her.

Lastly, think about your hands and face together. How often do you touch your face while talking? Also think about what you do with your hands when you're communicating with someone. The use of your hands can signal deceit, anxiety, or boredom (Fradet, n.d.). Following are some of those behaviors.

- Checking your watch
- Picking lint off your clothing (or pretending to)
- Tapping your fingers
- Rubbing your chin
- Placing your hand on your cheek
- Placing your hand over your mouth
- Fidgeting

Arms

When examining body language, arms don't usually come to mind right away. But your arms can communicate lots of messages, such as giving off signs of comfort, discomfort, or confidence (Navarro, 2008).

Traditionally, people have seen crossing the arms as defensive, insecure, or maybe even uninterested. Some people may argue that crossing your arms makes you feel more comfortable, however: "Any gesture will feel comfortable when you have the corresponding attitude; that is, if you have a negative, defensive, or nervous attitude, folded arms will feel comfortable" (Navarro, 2008, p. 92). In addition, think about when you're in a fun situation like being at a party with your friends—do you cross your arms then? Chances are you don't. Regardless of how comfortable you may feel when you cross your arms, you have to be aware of the negative message it sends to your audience. Therefore, avoid it. Pease and Pease (2006) suggest holding something like a pen to force you to unfold your arms and maybe even lean forward into the conversation, which would communicate a completely different message. On the other hand, avoid holding items in front of you like a barrier between you and your audience (such as purses, bags, or coffee mugs).

Sometimes the arm crossing is more of a self-hug. Body language expert Joe Navarro (2014) outlines some messages the self-hug communicates with people. The first is stress relief. People typically use self-hug arm crossing to provide comfort. So, if that is the case, then it's natural to use your arms to self-hug when you are in a stressful situation to relax and calm down. Navarro (2014) also states that people use self-hugs to hide their insecurities—maybe they feel the need to cover their mid-section or a top they are wearing. Either way, it does not convey confidence.

You can communicate positive messages using your arms when you leave them open. You can put them up in the air, such as at a sporting event when your team scores in overtime, or by keeping them at your side, such as while sitting in a meeting to show you are friendly and approachable.

Feet and Legs

Navarro (2008) states that the body parts most likely to communicate your honest feelings or thoughts are actually your feet and legs. He explains this by saying that before humans could speak, our feet and legs responded to threats immediately without much thought:

> This ability to communicate nonverbally has assured our survival as a species, and even though today we often cover our legs with clothing and our feet with shoes, our lower limbs still react—not only to threats and stressors—but also to emotions, both negative and positive. (Navarro, 2008, p. 55)

Feet

The good news is that not a lot of people are going to look at your feet, so it's easier to ignore them, but with body language, it's still a good idea to be aware of *all* messages, including those that certain positions and gestures of your feet can communicate.

Pointing your feet toward someone signals that you are interested in what they are saying—so consider this when you stop in the hallway to talk to someone. While you're facing that person, which way are your feet pointed? If one foot is pointed in the other direction, that communicates disinterest. Tapping your feet can communicate impatience. But crossing your feet can show that you are comfortable. Navarro (2008) states, "When you cross one leg in front of the other while standing, you reduce your balance significantly. . . . For this reason, the limbic [instinctual] brain allows us to perform this behavior only when we feel comfortable or confident" (p. 69).

Legs

When considering legs, think about how you stand or sit. Standing and sitting are another way to communicate unintended messages to your staff. First, let's look at sitting and what your posture is like when you sit. Slouching communicates insecurity or even inattentiveness. While sitting, shaking your legs can communicate anxiety, nervousness, or boredom—so either way, avoid doing so. When crossing your legs while sitting, Navarro (2008) says to pay attention to any barriers between you and the other people at the table. For example, when you cross your leg over the other one, is your knee significantly high up so it acts as a barrier? Or do you cross your legs so that your ankle is over your thigh, taking up a lot of space—which communicates arrogance?

While standing, think about how close you stand to people. Most people need personal space, so when you end up standing too close to people, you are most likely making them feel uncomfortable. At work, your communications with your staff or stakeholders should occur at about four to nine feet away—which Glenn Wilson (2016) calls the *business zone*. The *social zone* or *friendship zone* is a distance of about eighteen inches to four feet. Don't forget to be sensitive to possible cultural differences when it comes to personal space.

Dress to Impress

Whether you like it or not, your appearance is a component of body language. Wilson (2016) says, "We are often told not to judge a book by its cover. Yet that is precisely what we do a lot of the time. We sum up others at a glance by the way they are dressed and presented" (p. 23). The way you dress can communicate your position of authority, or how you value yourself. It communicates your self-confidence. As a school leader, you should always dress like a school leader. Think about going in for an interview; you dress to impress, right? You dress for whatever position you are interviewing for and there's a reason for that. Once you get that position, continue to dress in that manner. Wearing dirty or wrinkled clothing can communicate a negative message about you because your appearance tells your staff, students, and parents how much you value yourself.

Accessories, makeup, and hairstyles are also a part of your body language because again, like your clothing, they say a lot about how you value yourself. This form of body language shows that you are important and that you take yourself seriously. And when you take yourself seriously, your staff, parents, and students will take you seriously. When you show that you respect yourself, your staff, parents, and students will show you respect. Read more about personal appearance on page 21.

Observing Body Language

Considering the different body language cues you have just read about—your face, arms, hands, feet, legs, and appearance—what have you learned about your own body language? A great technique to become self-aware of your body language is to observe other people and their body language. Make the connection of what it communicates to you. Use the reproducible "Body Language Look-Fors in Others" (page 128) to observe people around you—either in your school or outside your school. As you observe people, jot down all the different body language cues you see in their faces, arms, hands, feet, legs, and overall look. Then record what that body language communicates to you. This will help you become more aware of your own body language and what your body language may communicate to others.

Elements of Effective Body Language

Many times, your body language communicates your emotions. Think about times when you have been angry, frustrated, excited, or sad. No matter how hard you may try to keep these emotions hidden, they can come out in body language. "Body language is an outward reflection of a person's emotional condition" (Pease & Pease, 2006, p. 11). Use the reproducible "Body Language Indicators for Emotions" (page 129) to record your body language when you experience certain emotions so you're aware of how you communicate nonverbally.

It is not wise to hide or suppress your emotions—instead think about how you can try to control them. Of course, you are human, and there are days when you will be upset or frustrated at something or someone. But as a leader, you must learn to control your emotions. Otherwise, when you communicate negative emotions through your body language, it can jeopardize whatever message you are trying to convey verbally. Harvey Deutschendorf (2016, 2019) offers leaders the following five suggestions to help them control their emotions.

1. Be self-aware.
2. Share appropriately.
3. Manage your mood.
4. Take time to respond, instead of react.
5. Look for solutions instead of blame.

Be Self-Aware

Effective leaders understand what causes certain emotions. Knowing this means you can control those triggers. More importantly, it's important to never react or make decisions while you are in that emotional state. And when you are, know what you need to do in order to become neutral (for example, breathing techniques, exercise, and so on).

Share Appropriately

Effective leaders know how to share their emotions appropriately. You can use this opportunity to connect with your staff and stakeholders by sharing how you feel— but staying in control. For example, if a first-year teacher on your staff shares with you that he or she is struggling with classroom management and at times is getting very frustrated, you can share how you felt when you first began your career to help connect with this teacher and build trust.

Manage Your Mood

Effective leaders are aware of their own mood swings and able to put these aside while at work because the focus is on the work. For example, almost all of us have walked into school to begin our day in a bad mood. Maybe the bad mood is a result of your favorite sports teaming losing the championship game the night before, maybe you just woke up not feeling well, maybe you got into a fight with your spouse that morning—the possibilities are endless. Whatever put you in a bad mood that day, you must know and understand that everyone in the school is depending on you to be focused and to lead, which means you have to be able to manage it.

Take Time to Respond, Instead of React

When we react immediately, we may elicit an emotional response. But if you take time to think and process the issue at hand before responding, chances are your response will be a much more effective one. That time you take to respond allows you to engage your thinking processes, which will result in better decisions. For example, say that a teacher who you have talked to about coming to work on time is late again. Instead of reacting to the behavior in frustration, and possibly antagonizing him or her, take the time to think through how and what you will say. A measured response stands a much better chance of getting that teacher to improve his or her tardiness issues.

Look for Solutions Instead of Blame

Effective leaders always look for solutions because when you get stuck on blaming others, you are naturally going to cause emotional reactions. For example, if an initiative does not yield the positive results you were hoping for, it can be really easy to blame the teachers. But when you do that, you help no one because not only will you have a negative emotional response, so will your teachers. When you're focused on solutions, your emotions are neutral because you are trying to resolve the issue instead of being mad or upset with someone.

Body Language for Leaders

Now that you have reviewed all the different ways you can communicate through your body language, let's take a look at some simple tips and strategies that you can make a conscious effort to use in order to communicate that you are a strong, confident leader.

- Make eye contact.
- Smile.
- Give firm handshakes.
- Dress professionally.

- Maintain a straight posture.
- Use open gestures (arms open, hands open, palms facing up, and so on).
- Avoid self-soothing gestures (playing with hair, tapping your fingers, hugging yourself, and so on).
- Cultivate emotional intelligence.

This list only skims the surface of the many things you can do to strengthen your communication via body language. See the reproducible "The Dos and Don'ts of Body Language Communication" (page 130), which you can use to self-reflect on what you specifically need to do (and perhaps stop doing) to ensure you communicate like a strong, confident leader through your body language.

Summary

It's easy to miss the impact body language can have on you as a leader. How you communicate nonverbally can damage or strengthen your verbal messages, and more importantly, it can damage or strengthen your relationships with all the people you are leading. Again, as I mentioned at the beginning of this chapter, communication is so much more than just words. Think of all the messages you communicate nonverbally using your eyes, arms, hands, feet, and legs. Think of what you communicate through how you dress. Think of the emotions that are evident through your body language. It is imperative that you are aware of your body language so that you can communicate what you want to communicate nonverbally.

Reflection Questions ↩

1. Why should you be aware of body language communication?
2. How can your body language build trust with your staff, parents, and students?
3. How can you increase your emotional intelligence so that you can communicate effectively through your body language?
4. What is your body language weakness? In other words, what do you do that you know is not what you want to communicate?

The School Leader's Communication Challenge: Body Language

The following challenge is designed to be flexible. Use it to be mindful of your body language in interactions with others throughout the month, and if you have an important interaction, meeting, or presentation that you know is coming up, you can use these resources to prepare.

Challenge	Notes
• Show interest in conversations by maintaining eye contact. • Control your emotions. • Use the reproducible "Body Language Look-Fors in Others" (page 128) to help you reflect on how body language can enhance communication. • Fill out the reproducible "Body Language Indicators for Emotions" (page 129) to help you analyze your own body language. • Use the reproducible "The Dos and Don'ts of Body Language Communication" (page 130) to determine what you need to do more of and what you need to stop. • Conduct the SWOT analysis (page 131) and monitor your goal.	

REPRODUCIBLE

Body Language Look-Fors in Others

Observe and list the body language of people around you and then reflect on what it communicates to you.

Body Language Observed	What It Might Communicate

Body Language Indicators for Emotions

List all the ways your body language could communicate the corresponding emotion.

Emotion	Body Language Indicators
Disappointed	
Angry	
Frustrated	
Confused	
Nervous	
Stressed	
Bored	
Remorseful	
Happy	
Calm	

Connecting Through Leadership © 2020 Solution Tree Press • SolutionTree.com
Visit **go.SolutionTree.com/leadership** to download this free reproducible.

The Dos and Don'ts of Body Language Communication

Reflect on your own facial expressions, hands, arms, legs, and feet, as well as how you dress. What do you know you need to do, and what should you stop doing?

As a Leader, I Should . . .	As a Leader, I Should Never . . .

SWOT Analysis on My Body Language

Strengths	Weaknesses	Opportunities	Threats
What are your strengths as they relate to your body language?	What are your weaknesses as they relate to your body language?	How can you get better at communicating what you want to communicate through your body language?	Think of ways your body language could be misinterpreted. How can you prevent them?

My goal for improving my body language:

Afterword

*Developing excellent communication skills
is absolutely essential to effective leadership.
The leader must be able to share knowledge
and ideas to transmit a sense of urgency and
enthusiasm to others. If a leader can't get a
message across clearly and motivate others
to act on it, then having a message doesn't
even matter.*

—Gilbert Amelio

The purpose of this book is not only to educate school leaders on the importance of effective communication but also to provide you with tips and strategies to help strengthen your communication skills in order to effectively lead your schools. Without skills, it is nearly impossible to lead effectively. Your job as school leader requires you to communicate well every day. You communicate every time you have a conversation, including the tough ones. You communicate every time you make a presentation. You communicate every time you facilitate a meeting. You communicate every time you write an email or a newsletter. You communicate every time and all the time through your body language. And in all these situations, you are conveying a variety of messages, such as a message that is inspiring and motivating your stakeholders, or a message that is direct, or a message that is influential. The success of your leadership depends on you communicating messages effectively.

Every chapter in this book begins with a quote. I invite you now to flip back through the book and take another look at each quote in turn. What does each one mean to you? What implications do any or all of them have for you as a school leader?

Communication is essential to effective leadership. It is through communication that you are able to achieve what it is that you want to achieve. Whatever legacy you want to leave behind as a school leader, effective communication will be its vehicle.

In order for your message to be received the way you intend, you must be able to communicate and connect with your audience effectively, thereby building trust. After you take the communication challenge, hopefully you will see an improvement in your communication skills. Even after the challenge, continue to monitor and be aware of your communication skills to keep improving them; this will help you be the best school leader you can be.

References and Resources

American Management Association. (2015). *9 things you should never do when giving a presentation: AMA research.* Accessed at https://playbook.amanet .org/9-things-never-giving-presentation/ on May 6, 2019.

Anderson, C. (2016). *TED talks: The official TED guide to public speaking.* Toronto, ON: HarperCollins Canada.

Atkinson, C. (2005). *Beyond bullet points: Using Microsoft PowerPoint to create presentations that inform, motivate and inspire.* Redmond, WA: Microsoft Press.

Axtell, P. (2018). The most productive meetings have fewer than 8 people. *Harvard Business Review.* Accessed at https://hbr.org/2018/06/the-most -productive-meetings-have-fewer-than-8-people on September 19, 2019.

Bailey, S. (2013). *Just say no: How your meeting habit is harming you.* Accessed at www.forbes .com/sites/sebastianbailey/2013/08/08/just-say-no-how-your -meeting-habit-is-harming-you/#4bf73e411cfa on April 30, 2019.

Bang, H., Fuglesang, S., Ovesen, M. R., & Eilertsen, D. E. (2010). Effectiveness in top management group meetings: The role of goal clarity, focused communication, and learning behavior. *Scandinavian Journal of Psychol*ogy, *51*(3), 253–261.

Barrett, D. J. (2014). *Leadership communication* (4th ed.). New York: McGraw-Hill Education.

Baude, D.-M. (2007). *The executive guide to e-mail correspondence: Including model letters for every situation.* Franklin Lakes, NJ: Career Press.

Bonaccio, S., O'Reilly, J., O'Sullivan, S. L., & Chiocchio, F. (2016). Nonverbal behavior and communication in the workplace: A review and an agenda for research. *Journal of Management, 42*(5), 1044–1074.

Booher, D. (2017). *Communicate like a leader: Connecting strategically to coach, inspire, and get things done.* Oakland, CA: Berrett-Koehler.

Brooks, M. (2017). *10 reasons why business writing skills are so important.* Accessed at www .businessworld.ie/news/10-Reasons-Why-Business-Writing-Skills -Are-So-Important-569924.html on April 30, 2019.

Burnison, G. (2012). *The twelve absolutes of leadership.* New York: McGraw-Hill.

Butler, A. S. (2014). *Mission critical meetings: 81 practical facilitation techniques.* Tucson, AZ: Wheatmark.

Cabane, O. F. (2012). *The charisma myth: How anyone can master the art and science of personal magnetism.* New York: Penguin.

de Bono, E. (1985). *Six thinking hats.* New York: Little, Brown.

DeLoatch, P. (2015). *The 25 best school websites.* Accessed at https://schoolleadership20.com/forum/topics/the-25-best-school-websites-by-pamela-deloatch?overrideMobileRedirect=1 on September 19, 2019.

Deutschendorf, H. (2016). *Five ways the most effective leaders manage their emotions.* Accessed at www.fastcompany.com/3063692/five-ways-the-most-effective-leaders-manage-their-emotions on September 8, 2019.

Deutschendorf, H. (2019). *7 ways emotionally intelligent people handle workplace pressure.* Accessed at www.fastcompany.com/90385601/7-ways-emotionally-intelligent-people-handle-workplace-pressure on September 7, 2019

DuFour, R., DuFour, R., Eaker, R., Many, T. W., & Mattos, M. (2016). *Learning by doing. A handbook for Professional Learning Communities at Work* (3rd ed.). Bloomington, IN: Solution Tree Press.

DuFour, R., & Fullan, M. (2013). *Cultures built to last: Systemic PLCs at Work.* Bloomington, IN: Solution Tree Press.

Eisenbart, B., Garbuio, M., Mascia, D., & Morandi, F. (2016). Does scheduling matter? When unscheduled decision making results in more effective meetings. *Journal of Strategy and Management, 9*(1), 15–38.

Ekman, P. (1977). Facial expressions. In A. W. Siegman & S. Feldstein (Eds.), *Nonverbal behavior and communication* (pp. 97–116). Hillsdale, NJ: Erlbaum.

Espy, L. (2017). *Bad meetings happen to good people: How to run meetings that are effective, focused, and produce results.* Memphis, TN: Blue Room Press.

Fetzer, J. (2009). Quick, efficient, effective? Meetings! *Analytical and Bioanalytical Chemistry, 393*(8), 1825–1827.

Forde, J. (2017). *Why you need an employee handbook and what it should cover.* Accessed at www.tlnt.com/why-you-need-an-employee-handbook-and-what-it-should-cover/ on May 2, 2019.

Fradet, N. (n.d.). *13 revealing body language hand gestures.* Accessed at https://nicolasfradet.com/hand-body-language/ on May 2, 2019.

Gallo, C. (2017). *Presentation secrets of Steve Jobs: How to be insanely great in front of any audience.* New York: McGraw-Hill.

Garner, E. (2012). *The art of communicating: 500 quotes on how to communicate with others.* Accessed at www.cbscouting.com/resources/the-art-of-communicating.pdf on September 19, 2019.

Goman, C. K. (2011a). *Shaking hands—Body language at work.* Accessed at www.forbes.com/sites/carolkinseygoman/2011/09/28/shaking-hands-body-language-at-work on May 2, 2019.

Goman, C. K. (2011b). *The silent language of leaders: How body language can help or hurt how you lead.* San Francisco: Jossey-Bass.

Goman, C. K. (2018). *5 ways body language impacts leadership results.* Accessed at www.forbes.com/sites/carolkinseygoman/2018/08/26/5-ways-body-language-impacts-leadership-results on September 8, 2019.

Goodman, A., & Cause Communications. (2006). *Why bad presentations happen to good causes: And how to ensure they won't happen to yours.* Los Angeles: Cause Communications.

Harkins, P. (2017). *Powerful conversations: How high-impact leaders communicate* (2nd ed.). New York: McGraw-Hill Education.

Heflebower, T. (2019). *Presenting perfected: Feedback, tips, tricks, and troubleshooting.* New Providence, NJ: Bowker.

Kafele, B. K. (2015). *The principal 50: Critical leadership questions for inspiring schoolwide excellence.* Alexandria, VA: Association for Supervision and Curriculum Development.

Kanold, T. D. (2011). *The five disciplines of PLC leaders.* Bloomington, IN: Solution Tree Press.

Kaps, R. W., & Voges, J. K. (2007). Nonverbal communications: A commentary on body language in the aviation teaching environment. *The Journal of Aviation/Aerospace Education and Research, 17*(1), 43–52.

Kessler, A. (2015, January 1). Let's call off the meeting and get back to work. *The Wall Street Journal.* Accessed at www.wsj.com/articles/andy-kessler-lets-call-off-the-meeting-and-get-back-to-work-1420156148 on May 3, 2019.

Lamb, S. E. (2011). *How to write it: A complete guide to everything you'll ever write* (3rd ed.). New York: Ten Speed Press.

Lunenburg, F. C. (2010). Louder than words: The hidden power of nonverbal communication in the workplace. *International Journal of Scholarly Academic Intellectual Diversity, 12*(1), 1–5.

Luong, A., & Rogelberg, S. G. (2005). Meetings and more meetings: The relationship between meeting load and the daily well-being of employees. *Group Dynamics: Theory, Research, and Practice, 9*(1), 58–67.

Luthra, A., & Dahiya, R. (2015). Effective leadership is all about communicating effectively: Connecting leadership and communication. *International Journal of Management and Business Studies, 5*(3), 43–48.

MacLeod, L. (2011). Conducting a well-managed meeting. *Physician Executive, 37*(6), 80–85.

Mankins, M., Brahm, C., & Caimi, G. (2014, May). Your scarcest resource. *Harvard Business Review.* Accessed at https://hbr.org/2014/05/your-scarcest-resource on May 3, 2019.

Maxwell, J. C. (1993). *Developing the leader within you.* Nashville, TN: Thomas Nelson.

Medina, J. (2008). *Brain rules: 12 principles for surviving and thriving at work, home, and school.* Seattle, WA: Pear Press.

Muckian, M., & Woods, J. (1996). *The business letter handbook: How to write effective letters and memos for every business situation.* Avon, MA: Adams Media.

Murray, K. (2013). *The language of leaders: How top CEOs communicate to inspire, influence and achieve results* (2nd ed.). Philadelphia: Kogan Page.

Navarro, J. (2008). *What every body is saying: An ex-FBI agent's guide to speed-reading people.* New York: HarperCollins.

Navarro, J. (2014, October 6). *9 truths exposing a myth about body language* [Blog post]. Accessed at www.psychologytoday.com/us/blog/spycatcher/201410/9-truths-exposing-myth-about-body-language on May 3, 2019.

Nowak, A. (2004). *Power speaking: The art of the exceptional public speaker.* New York: Allworth Press.

Pachter, B., & Cowie, D. (2017). *The communication clinic: 99 proven cures for the most common business mistakes*. New York: McGraw-Hill.

Patel, D. S. (2014). Body language: An effective communication tool. *The IUP Journal of English Studies, 9*(2), 90–95.

Patterson, K., Grenny, J., McMillan, R., & Switzler, A. (2002). *Crucial conversations: Tools for talking when stakes are high*. New York: McGraw-Hill.

Pease, A., & Pease, B. (2006). *The definitive book of body language: The hidden meaning behind people's gestures and expressions*. New York: Bantam Dell.

Perlow, L. A., Hadley, C. N., & Eun, E. (2017, July–August). Stop the meeting madness. *Harvard Business Review*. Accessed at https://hbr.org/2017/07/stop-the-meeting -madness on May 3, 2019.

Pietrucha, F. J. (2014). *Supercommunicator: Explaining the complicated so anyone can understand*. New York: American Management Association.

Rehn, A. (2016). *The 20-minute rule for great public speaking—on attention spans and keeping focus*. Accessed at https://medium.com/the-art-of-keynoting/the-20-minute-rule-for -great-public-speaking-on-attention-spans-and-keeping-focus-7370cf06b636 on May 6, 2019.

Roman, K., & Raphaelson, J. (2000). *Writing that works: How to communicate effectively in business, e-mail, letters, memos, presentations, plans, reports, proposals, resumes, speeches* (3rd ed.). New York: Quill.

Romano, N. C., & Nunamaker, J. F. (2001). Meeting analysis: Findings from research and practice. In *Proceedings of the Thirty-Fourth Annual Hawaii International Conference on System Sciences*. Accessed at http://citeseerx.ist.psu.edu/viewdoc/download?doi=10.1.1 .570.6650&rep=rep1&type=pdf on May 6, 2019.

Scott, S. (2004). *Fierce conversations: Achieving success at work and in life, one conversation at a time*. New York: Berkley.

Umoh, R. (2018). *These 5 simple body language tricks can help you build trust with anyone*. Accessed at www.cnbc.com/2018/08/07/5-simple-body-language -tricks-to-build-trust-with-anyone.html on September 5, 2019.

Vjestica, I. (2012). *5 classic presentation fonts*. Accessed at https://thepresentationdesigner. co.uk/5-classic-presentation-fonts on September 19, 2019.

Weissman, J. (2004). *Absolute beginner's guide to winning presentations*. Indianapolis, IN: Que.

Weissman, J. (2009). *Presenting to win: The art of telling your story* (Updated and expanded ed.). Upper Saddle River, NJ: Pearson Education.

Wertheim, E. G. (n.d.). *The importance of effective communication*. Accessed at https://ysrinfo .files.wordpress.com/2012/06/effectivecommunication5.pdf on May 6, 2019.

Williams, A. (2017). *6 ways hesitant leaders can embrace social media*. Accessed at www .businessnewsdaily.com/7370-social-leadership.html on May 6, 2019.

Wilson, G. (2016). *Body language: The signals you don't know you're sending, and how to master them*. London: Icon.

Worrall, D. (2013). *Accountability leadership: How great leaders build a high performance culture of accountability and responsibility*. Carlton, NSW: Worrall & Associates.

Index

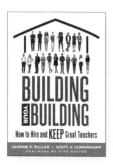

Building Your Building
Jasmine K. Kullar and Scott A. Cunningham
A growing teacher attrition rate, combined with fewer teachers entering the profession, has created a teacher shortage in many schools. In *Building Your Building*, the authors detail how school administrators can overcome these challenges to ensure they hire—and retain—great teachers.
BKF896

Crafting Your Message
Tammy Heflebower (with Jan Hoegh)
Become a confident, dynamic presenter with the guidance of *Crafting Your Message*. Written by expert presenter Tammy Heflebower, this book outlines a clear process for planning and delivering highly effective presentations. More than 100 ideas and strategies help you augment your message.
BKF931

Messaging Matters
William D. Parker
Harness the power of messaging to create a culture of acknowledgment, respect, and celebration. Written specially for leaders, this title is divided into three parts, helping readers maximize their role as chief communicators with students, teachers, and parents and community.
BKF785

Lead From the Start
Tommy Reddicks and Tina Merriweather Seymour
Lead From the Start will help brand-new principals and experienced leaders in new jobs succeed in their role. Veteran principals outline how to quickly develop best practices and systems that ensure better outcomes for your students, staff, and school.
BKF924

Visit SolutionTree.com or call 800.733.6786 to order.

GLOBAL PD

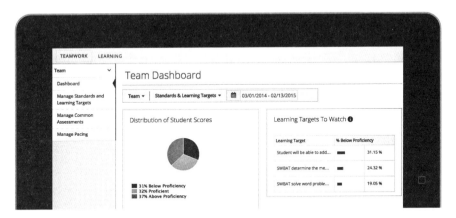

The **Power to Improve**
Is in Your Hands

Global PD gives educators focused and goals-oriented training from top experts. You can rely on this innovative online tool to improve instruction in every classroom.

- Get unlimited, on-demand access to guided video and book content from top Solution Tree authors.

- Improve practices with personalized virtual coaching from PLC-certified trainers.

- Customize learning based on skill level and time commitments.

▶ **REQUEST A FREE DEMO TODAY**
SolutionTree.com/GlobalPD

Solution Tree